*Women Called To Lead*

Fielding University Press is an imprint of Fielding Graduate University.

Its objective is to advance the research and scholarship of Fielding faculty, students and alumni around the world, using a variety of publishing platforms. For more information, please contact Fielding University Press, attn. Greta Walters, 2020 De la Vina Street, Santa Barbara, CA 93105. Phone: (805) 898-2924. Fax: (805) 690-4310. On the web: www.fielding.edu.

© Fielding Graduate University, 2017

Published in the United States of America by Fielding University Press

Library of Congress Cataloging-in-Publication data

Women Called to Lead

1. Education systems – higher learning.

# Women Called to Lead

Edited by

Kimarie Engerman, PhD

Stephanie Luster-Teasley, PhD

Christa Ellen Washington, PhD

Olga Bolden-Tiller, PhD

Foreword by Kelly Mack, PhD

# DEDICATION

*To Orlando Taylor for calling us to lead.*

# Table of Contents

# FOREWORD

## by Kelly M. Mack, Ph.D.

Today we know and understand more about effective leadership than ever before. Countless articles, books, and Internet blogs now explain and promote different kinds of leadership in ways that couldn't have been imagined just a few years ago. However, few of these accepted theories fully capture the leader skillset that is unique to women of color. The "added dimension" that they intuitively bring to solving complex problems and negotiating infrastructural barriers is all but absent in mainstream definitions of leadership. Further, research studies of successful leaders rarely include examples of women, let alone women of color, and their lived experiences; and even fewer include women of color in STEM.

One can easily argue that there are relatively fewer women of color in academic STEM leadership positions. Indeed, many reports have identified their significant dearth, particularly at the presidential level. What is particularly alarming about the reporting of statistics such as these is the seeming naiveté or complete denial of many in STEM higher education reform who fail to connect the underrepresentation of women of color in STEM with the diminished capacity of our nation to meet its Broadening Participation mandate. Not only do women of color as leaders in the academic STEM enterprise serve as professional role models for all underrepresented STEM students but, more importantly, they deeply understand the intricacies of the kind of proven methodological and practical approaches to institutional change that lead to full participation in the academic STEM disciplines. The complexity of the lived experience at the intersection of race and gender makes women of color uniquely poised to offer to the entire STEM enterprise more sophisticated ways of asking questions and producing new methods of creating and interpreting knowledge.

Therefore, at a time such as this in our nation's history—when threats to our global preeminence in science and technology loom so large—we simply cannot afford to continue to allow the potential power of women of color in academic STEM leadership to be seen as indistinct. To do so would not only dishonor our beloved STEM disciplines that rely upon an infusion of diverse perspectives for the technological and medical advances we enjoy today, but would also rob our students of the fully inclusive and optimally effective educational experiences they so deserve.

*Women Called to Lead* offers us an authentic perspective on leadership by women of color in the academic STEM disciplines. It captures a narrative of leadership that is based in ingenuity, tenacity, creativity, and grace. Whether it is an institutional change initiative, campus advising improvements, or data analytics, this book keenly focuses on a cadre of leaders with innate talents and capacities to see beyond statistics to underlying stories, identify unseen potentials, and reason beyond deficit models of thinking—all in order to achieve institutional change. While you probably won't ever find these particular combinations of leadership characteristics highlighted in major publications, they are nevertheless critical to ensuring that access to and preparedness for a

STEM degree is, and remains, a fundamental right for all.

Whether you are already a leader in STEM higher education reform, or considering becoming one, this is the book for you. In it, you will be inspired and awakened to an entirely different view of what effective leadership actually looks like when the perspective of the non-dominant group is unmasked. In this book, several STEM women of color chronicle their leadership experiences. They offer us an untethered look into their inspirations and motivations for leadership. Their courage, openness, and candor serve as an incredible gift to STEM higher education reform, and to the nation at large. Here, if we care to look deeply enough, these women have provided us with a clear blueprint for designing the kind of STEM leadership development that will safeguard our nation's global competitiveness in science and technology.

**Kelly M. Mack, PhD**

*Vice President for Undergraduate STEM Education Executive Director, Project Kaleidoscope*

*Association of American Colleges and Universities*

# Introduction

## *Unlimited Possibilities: Strategies to Maintain Balance and Keep Your Sanity During Your Path to Leadership*

Stephanie Luster-Teasley, PhD

No matter how far women progress in their careers, we all fall victim to the voice that convinces us we are not able to achieve a goal. Sometimes it is an internal voice that can cause self-doubt or the excuses that we make to ourselves. It can even be the feeling that we are an "imposter." Otherwise known as *Imposter Syndrome*, it is when a woman falsely feels that despite her hard work and achievements, her success is based on luck (Frankel & Mitchell, 2005; Sandberg, 2013a; Sindermann, 2001). Doubt that limits us can also be the result of comments made by a person at work, our families, or within our professional community that make us second-guess ourselves and cause us to lean back as opposed to leaning into our careers (Burton, 2012; Sandberg, 2013b).

Women who want to become leaders are faced with the triple challenge of overcoming the intersectionality between gender, career, and family that adds an extra dynamic to understanding how to achieve career goals. Do you have a balance between teaching, research, and service? Are you getting the most return on your time investments for career progression? Are you working hard with little recognition as compared to your male counterparts? Is something in your personal life being neglected because you are too busy chasing after things that have little return on investment? If you are a minority woman, race may be an additional factor that affects your career (Rockquemore & Laszloffy, 2008). You may wonder if you are being judged, invited, or passed over for leadership opportunities because of gender or race. It is difficult to figure out which factors are significant and which are simply the "voice" that limits your unlimited potential. It is also confusing to decipher how students, colleagues, and staff perceive you when you are one of only a few women within your department or college unit. Thus, planning your career strategically and intentionally is essential.

## Establishing Your Mode of Operation

I am an associate professor at a doctoral granting university where I have worked for over 10 years. I have been fortunate to be successful at teaching, research, and service with recognition at national levels. As a faculty member, I am required to teach, research, and participate in service or engagement with the community. At my university, we have high teaching loads but must also demonstrate a high level of scholarship and grantsmanship. Early in my career, I realized I had a passion for teaching and outreach but research and grantsmanship were vital for career progression. I also realized that as a female in a predominately male field such as engineering, I needed to establish a "mode of operation" that provided a strategy for how to balance my career, my family, and my personal priorities.

The best advice I can give to other women who may be interested in leadership but are faced with the same challenges is that you must establish your own "rules for playing the game," or your "mode of operation." Your specific rules need to be unique to you and what your needs are professionally and personally; however, I am providing some general guidelines that may help you develop your plan to balance work and personal goals. My list is based on the role I have as a faculty member, wife, and mother of two boys.

## Prioritize what matters the most in your personal and professional career

For me, my family always comes first. I made this rule early in my career because I was a mother to two boys and my husband was finishing his MS degree in another state. Therefore, the day-to-day tasks largely fell on me. I also decided there were no excuses for not being prepared to teach my courses, because I wanted to be highly respected as an excellent educator. Additionally, as a young assistant professor I wanted to establish my research direction, but acknowledged that was a longer-term goal that I could take more time to develop. Quickly, I determined the order of importance and I clearly and consistently practiced these choices with my actions. I would revisit my priority list as I made decisions for which tasks needed to be done first. My short-term and long-term tasks were then prioritized based on the following: (1) things that needed to be done immediately; (2) things that could be delayed to the next day if I could not get to them that day; and (3) things that I could complete in the future. Family and teaching therefore were my initial priorities early in my career. Once my teaching became routine, my boys became more independent, and my husband finished his degree, I was able to shift my priorities so I could focus on my research. Therefore, identifying and strategically focusing on foundational priorities can transition into the ability to multitask and expand into new areas and goals.

## Smart multitasking to aggressively meet goals: teaching; research; service; and family

I love the opportunities academia provides for teaching, research, and service. Once I started on my path to my PhD, I knew I wanted to work at a minority-serving institution to help minority students become engineers. I now realize that, because I am one of only a handful of minority, females in our college, students seek my help and advice more than that of my male colleagues. Like most of my female faculty friends, I genuinely care about helping our students, but the time it takes for the additional service to students can leave you drained before you even have a chance to complete your teaching and research tasks. This is not to mention that, when you leave work, you may need to go home to your second and most important job—your family, your home, and yourself.

## Set operating rules and follow them

Setting rules leads to smart multitasking. You must set rules and boundaries that help you protect your time so that you can focus on completing your priorities. For example, before you undertake helping students or service, establish rules for how they can access you and your time. When you teach a large number of students, their concerns can overwhelm you and sidetrack you from your priority list. For example, as a rule of thumb, I only write recommendation letters on Thursdays. To receive a letter, the student must ask me in person and provide a hardcopy of their résumé with the information I need to be able to complete their letter. All of their information must be given to me by Wednesday at least five days before the due date. Having these "operating" rules teaches others how to treat you and keeps you from being overwhelmed. I also make it clear that I do not write letters during holiday breaks, which is the time I devote to my family and myself.

Determine a schedule that works for you. If possible, establish specific days where you teach and have office hours and establish specific days where you can focus on research or service. If blocking off days will not work, try blocking off established times. Involve a team to help with your activities, such as students who can learn from what you are doing in your classroom, research, or service. However, make sure your team members receive a significant return on their investment, too. My family is also part of my team. Countless times I have asked their opinions about teaching methods and research ideas I want to try. My boys also keep me updated on the latest technology trends that I can use in my classroom to teach my technology-savvy Millennial students. A few final suggestions are to close your door and even consider disconnecting from email for preset periods to give yourself personal and professional time. Resist the urge to answer the door, because that "knock" on the door can wait. Space and time are important to longevity and continued success.

## Leverage Your Passions Into Scholarly and Fundable Endeavors

I write grant proposals for my research, teaching, and outreach.

The focus for my proposals centers on improving teaching practices, advancing my engineering discipline research in environmental remediation, and outreach activities. Funding is available through federal agencies, industry, and private foundations. If you have an interest in grant writing as one of your service areas, I would suggest you seek out funding opportunities for projects that you will be passionate to lead. Make sure you serve as the PI on grants more than as a co-PI. Consider applying for small grants such as internal university funding, private foundations, contracts, or projects with a single deliverable that can lead to bigger grants and help build your reputation and experience at grant management. The more you write and review proposals, the better you get at the process.

## Unlimited Thinking: Do not settle for the "no" when it could be a "yes"

It is very important to identify your priorities and goals, and to think in an unlimited way. Do not give up on what seems to be a far-reaching goal or career opportunity by immediately thinking of why you cannot do it. If it is an opportunity for growth or for advancement, focus on ways to achieve it. Women can be hesitant and fear saying "yes" to opportunities and, by default, the opportunity becomes a "no." Just before I received tenure, I had the opportunity to take two of my graduate students to a national lab for 10 weeks during the summer. Completing the application was not the scariest part of the process. The scariest part was asking my husband if he would agree to handle our boys for 10 weeks by himself. I asked him before applying and he indicated that we would figure out how to make it work. I was awarded the research opportunity and it turned out to be an experience that completely transformed how I ran my research lab. My family loved visiting me for short trips and my boys now have a new perspective on how much I love them and my research. The personal benefit from this experience was the quiet time to focus on myself and my research and work on my portfolio to apply for promotion and tenure. It afforded me the time to reflect on my career accomplishments and space to re-center my mode of operation for the next phase of my work in academia.

## What is the Return on Investment (ROI)?

Women in academia may find themselves in high service jobs or jobs where they are assisting their department, college, and university operations in their careers before becoming full professors. Examples include director for a program, assistant chair, department chair, co-PI, or assistant dean. They become stuck in these roles year after year. Because the jobs are demanding, their research productivity and career progression can suffer. When working with students, women can quickly become burdened with heavier service. Helping students is important, but if teaching and research expectations to earn tenure and promotion are neglected in your portfolio, you will not be able to remain in a faculty position to be there to help students.

Female faculty should strive to establish a career that progresses to full professorship. Many universities are approaching the standard where all upper level and senior administrators must be full professors. This means if you let your career progression stall with activities that do not lead to the path of promotion, then your path to senior leadership can become limited. So when I ask you to consider the return on investment (ROI), I am referring to reviewing the return or the benefit of an activity based on the time, brainpower, and commitment you must make to the activity. I am not suggesting that you to say "no" to helping students or participating in university roles, but rather enter into them with an exit plan and have boundaries. Set a target time limit on a high service job with a plan to achieve your next job. Look at the ROI and maximize what you will learn in the role and how it can advance your career. Do not immediately say "yes" to every opportunity. Ask for time to think. Women who are known to be leaders and excellent faculty are asked to participate on many service committees and university projects. Emails and last minute requests will come in asking for our service and often we are quick to respond. Don't! Give yourself time to consider the invitation and evaluate the ROI. If the request needs an immediate response, then the request is last minute, is probably stressful, and the result of poor planning, which is probably something you need to avoid anyway. After evaluating the request and determining that it is one that fits with your priorities and return on investment, then say "yes," but be clear to the requestor about what you need in order to be successful.

## Quieting the negative comments and evaluating the source of the comment

Sometimes it is hard to receive criticism and negative comments. Before taking these comments personally, identify whether they arise from a legitimate concern that you need to address or if the "messenger" may be flawed. For example, a few years ago I was managing four grants and working hard. A colleague of mine came into my office to discuss a project he had that demonstrated little return on investment other than helping with his initiative. Because I told him I could not help him pursue his project, he told me I was not working hard enough and that I needed to work harder. I took it personally until I realized his comment was based on my not agreeing to do something he wanted me to do. If someone gives you advice or criticism that is beneficial and helps you, use it. If, however, someone gives you advice that clearly has an underlying motive be careful, because the "messenger" may not have your best interest at heart.

## Be protective of your time and with whom you share your energy

Energy vampires are real! You need all the energy you have to do the things that you need to do. Avoid repetitive discussions with others that you know will drain you of your energy. Be protective of your time to prevent getting distracted for longer periods than expected. Politely let the person know a specific time when you will need to redirect your energies. I tend to look at the clock on my computer and tell the person talking to me a specific time when I need to move on to my task. If you do not protect your time but instead get caught in an energy sink with an energy vampire, it prevents you from rebounding to your tasks quickly.

## Make sure your role is valued and you are not just part of the "we need a woman" or "we need a minority" quota (on teams, grants, branding, etc.)

When I was an assistant professor, I had a few experiences where colleagues would ask me to be a part of their proposals. Their motives, however, were not altruistic. They did not value the contributions I could provide as a researcher. Their intentions, whether intentional or subconscious, existed along the stereotypical roles that universities assign to women and minorities. Examples include serving as the minority student recruiter, K-12 outreach leader, student mentor, club advisor, or being present for the photo shoot to prove there is a minority female faculty member.

Sometimes they only wanted to be able to check off that, yes, the research team has a female representative or, yes, the team has a minority represented. The requests were not based on a real investment of my abilities and what I could contribute to the team or the project. Once the grant was funded, the role would only result in high obligations, with low recognition and low ROI.

## Strategic alliances: a team of mentors and sponsors

You need more than just one mentor; you need a mentoring team. Many people focus on finding one person that can provide all their mentoring needs to become a well-rounded professional on the fast track. However, you should have a team of mentors that can play different roles. You can link with mentors that can give you advice to be a better teacher, a better researcher, or a better writer. Mix and match mentors to learn best practices from those who excel in their particular areas and complement the skills you need to learn. There are many different types of mentors to consider. If you are a mother or planning to have children, find mentors who are mothers that balance family and career. Peer-mentors who are at the same level as you but who have perhaps figured out a few tricks that they can teach you about balance are invaluable and you can share your expertise with them, too. You should also be able to provide mentoring back to the mentors who help you, hence making it a dual-mentor/protégé symbiosis. Never rule out professional counselors and career coaches who can help provide an unbiased view of your current situation in your work and personal life. They can become sounding boards to help you figure out yourself, figure out others around you, and maintain some sanity throughout your career.

Sponsors are people who know your work and are in positions of influence at your university, your profession, or your community. These are the people who can recommend your name when leadership roles are available. Sponsors can be mentors but they are more than likely people who see you advancing in your career and want to help you continue.

## READ, READ, READ books that help you develop professionally

There is nothing like a good book. Many books are published specifically focusing on women, academia, and leadership. Of course, as you read them, use what you can and create your own mode of operation. Use the best practices that work for you and your situation. Leadership books are excellent ways to develop additional skills that can help you manage your time, your research team, and your day-to-day practices. When you think about it, a good book is available any time you are free and you never need to make an appointment!

## Finale: Your Path to Your Own Career, Family, and Personal Balance

It is difficult being a female in academia who has a lot of tasks to juggle. Although most people would say there is no real work-life balance, it is manageable. I think you can at least find the balance that works for you. Strive to leverage your passions with your career and personal goals, enjoy what you do, and do not compromise on your dreams. Determine how to strategically plan to reach your goals, and set the rules to balance work, home, and your personal happiness. I hope some of the advice I have provided here proves to be helpful but remember: no matter where your career takes you, make sure to always think unlimited!

## References

Burton, V. (2012). *Successful women think differently*. Eugene, OR: Harvest House Publishers.

Frankel, L. P., & Mitchell, H. (2005). *Nice girls don't get the corner office*. Time Warner AudioBooks.

Rockquemore, K., & Laszloffy, T. A. (2008). *The black academic's guide to winning tenure—without losing your soul*. Boulder, CO: Lynne Rienner Publishers.

Sandberg, S. (2013). *Lean in: women, work, and the will to lead*. New York, NY: Random House.

Sindermann, C. J. (2001). *Winning the games scientists play:*

*Strategies for enhancing your career in science.* New York, NY: Basic Books.

# Part I

# Personal Journey (or Authentic Leadership)

# Pathway to Authentic Leadership

Clytrice Watson, PhD

Everybody has a story to tell. Some are good, some are bad, and some are in between. Regardless, our individual stories are unique and relevant to who we are. Every challenge we face, every battle we fight, every triumph we experience serves a critical role in our personal and professional development and self-discovery. As children, we have no control over our life circumstances, but as we grow into adulthood we have the privilege of making decisions related to our individual destiny. I chose to trust in God and the divine plan over my life, thus taking an active role in the development of my story. I am honored to share a small portion with you.

## Invisible

People have always told me what I couldn't do and what I wouldn't be and had no problems spewing out negativity over my life. Looking back, it seemed as if I had a bullseye on my chest for anyone to throw a dart of negativity right in the middle. When I was nine years old, one of my mother's friends looked at me and asked "Where were you when the pretties were being passed out?" I remember hunching my shoulders and responding, "I don't know." I guess it was at that point that I decided to hide from the world, meaning I tried not to be seen or heard. I figured if I just stayed out of people's way, no one would notice me. I tried to become invisible. This worked for a while, but not for long as that bullseye on my chest seemed to just keep growing and the at-tackers just kept attacking. It's bad enough to grow up in poverty and in a society that does not have much hope or expectations for you, but to constantly have to battle with emotional, physical, and psychological abuse is just too much for a young girl to handle. I screamed for help but no one heard me, and I acted out but no one saw me. To some extent, the shield of invisibility that I tried to create was effective.

At some point during my twelfth year of life, I started plan-ning the great escape from the life that I knew. At fifteen, I made a conscious decision not to become a statistic, but I still didn't have a clue how I was going to do this. I felt like Dorothy, the Coward-ly Lion, the heartless Tin Man and the Scarecrow, all trying to get to the Great Wizard for the answers. I needed to find my yellow brick road.

## Following the Yellow Brick Road

The yellow brick road started on the campus of the University of Maryland Eastern Shore (UMES) with the Upward Bound pro-gram when I was sixteen years old. Everything changed for me and I was on my way to the land of Oz. Whatever or wherever that was, for the first time ever, I was excited.

I started making strides, as I was the first of six children to graduate from high school without becoming a teenage mother and would become the first in my family to attend a four-year college. I really didn't understand the magnitude of this accom-plishment at the time because all I wanted to do was graduate from high school and get away from the horrid little town I grew up in. I was looking forward to starting a new life on the campus of Norfolk State University (NSU). My dreams were becoming a reality and I was more determined than ever to get to Oz, whatever and wherever that might be. I entered college with the intent of pursuing a medical degree. I graduated in four years, but not without some bumps and bruises along the way. The medical school thing did not work out so well. So I, along with my bruised ego, went back home and later enrolled in graduate school at Delaware State University (DSU). DSU accepted me when it seemed that no other place wanted me and little did I know that my time there would chart the course for my future.

## Fork in the Road

In order to pay for graduate school, I accepted a teaching assistantship. I had never entertained the idea of teaching, especially after a year of substitute teaching after college. I had concluded that anyone who became a teacher was completely out of their mind, but the experience I had change my life forever. Although my students were not much younger than I, I earned their respect through my willingness to help them and to not prejudge them. After all, it was only five years prior that I had been in their position, a first-generation college student who was pursuing her dream of obtaining a college education. I could certainly relate to their struggles. The pivotal moment for me was tutoring a young man (whom I will call Andre) in biology. He was struggling in this class, but it didn't seem as if he was really putting forth effort. One day I just laid into him about being lazy and not putting forth the effort to pass this class. The way he looked at me, I thought he was going to hit me, but instead he said, "I never had anyone come at me like that," and he started putting more effort into the class. At that point, I realized that teaching was not just about the transfer of information, but about motivating, inspiring, and pushing young people to be their best. But I still was not sure of what I was going to do with my life.

## Touched by an Angel

The funny thing about life is that you never know what to expect, and I had no idea that the yellow brick road was about to make a U-turn. As I left DSU with a master's degree in biology and my newly discovered talent for teaching, I was also planning a wedding, looking for a job, and dreaming about the house with the white picket fence. Little did I know that there was a divine plan being orchestrated for me as I literally walked into a job at the University of Maryland Eastern Shore. Keep in mind that this is where my yellow brick road began 10 years earlier. I was hired as an instructor of biology with the intention of only staying there for a maximum of two years, but before I knew it, I was enrolled in a PhD program. Why? I asked. You could say that I was touched by an angel, and her name is Dr. Carolyn Brooks. I first met her during the interview process, as she was the dean of the College of Agriculture and Natural Sciences. I thought I had met an angel because she was the most embracing and caring person that I had ever met. I cannot begin to articulate how I felt when I left her office, other than *awesome*! Dr. Brooks had a way of making you feel as if you were the only person that mattered at that moment and I had never met anyone like her before in my life. She became a "point of light" in my life and offered to serve as my PhD advisor. It was amazing for me to find that the land of Oz was at the very place my journey began and the Great Wizard was in fact a black woman.

The nine years I spent at UMES were incredible, as there were many ups and downs. My pathway to a PhD was nontraditional, considering I worked full time. At times I was somewhat unsure if this was really what I wanted to do, but I hung in there nonetheless. My position as an instructor was actually a split position that included administrative duties, and I later transitioned into a program coordinator's position, which was completely administrative. Needless to say, this allowed me to discover other unknown interests and talents, but balancing a family, work, and school was becoming overwhelming. I needed to make some decisions about pursuing this degree, and when a fellowship opportunity was presented to me I accepted. I relinquished my fulltime paycheck for a menial stipend in order to pursue my degree fulltime. The fear was immeasurable, but it was trumped by excitement at the idea of obtaining my terminal degree. Unfortunately, a number of life events happened that could have completely derailed me from this journey. These included my being diagnosed with multiple sclerosis, and my mother's death three days after the defense and approval of my dissertation proposal. Thankfully, I had a slew of friends and supporters to help me through this perilous period in my life. I had come to a fork in the road and I was really questioning my pursuit of perceived happiness via the PhD. I had slipped into a deep abyss of darkness and self-doubt, but thank God for those "points of light" that shone through my family, advisors, faculty, and peers. I graduated the following year and, as I prepared to walk across the stage, my mind was flooded with memories and emotions as I tried to accept that this was really happening. After all, I was that funny-looking black girl that no one really expected to do much in life. It was as if a mini-movie of my life was running in my head.

      ☐   I thought about the minister at my church who told me that I would be pregnant by the time I was 14. I was 13 at the time.

      ☐   I thought about the guidance counselor who advised me to enroll in the vocational program for cosmetology because I wasn't college material. I'm so glad my mother disagreed and said, "Yes, you are."

      ☐   I thought about the day I tried to take my own life by swallowing a bunch of pills. I'm glad I failed.

      ☐   I thought about my high school English teacher who taught me to use my pen to fight and not my fists. I was grateful that she cared.

      ☐   I thought about the Upward Bound director and the counselors that convinced me that I could go to college and showed me how to get there. I was so glad they believed in me.

      ☐   I thought about the college professors at Norfolk State University, who pushed me to work harder to pursue my dreams.

      ☐   I thought about the chairwoman of the biology department at Delaware State University, who invited me to enroll in the graduate program. I was grateful for the opportunity.

As I looked toward the stage into the eyes of my advisor,

I was overcome with emotions, thus realizing that I had indeed been touched by an angel. That day I knew the direction of my new journey.

## Fight or Flight

Once again, timing is everything. I visited the biology department at DSU and one of my former professors was now the chairperson. By coincidence, there was a faculty position available and he encouraged me to apply. Returning to one of my alma maters as a faculty member was truly an honor and I was eager to start this new chapter in my life. I admit it was strange to consider my former professors as my colleagues, but I was confident that they would provide the mentoring and support I needed to be successful. After all, I was a product of their teaching and training and certainly they would welcome one of their own back home. I was so naïve and unaware of the challenges that lurked in my future.

The demographics of the department consisted of two Caucasian women, one Egyptian woman, one African American man, two African men, five Caucasian men, and one black woman. Yes, that one black woman was me. Although I thought this was odd for an HBCU, it really didn't bother me at first, mainly because I was focused on doing the job and navigating through the academic ranks. By the end of my first year, I realized how underprepared I was for a faculty position. I really didn't have a full understanding of the promotion and tenure process; I had to start a research program from scratch; and I didn't know the ugly truth about academic politics. Most disappointing was learning that not all of my colleagues/former professors were excited about my hiring, which created a seemingly hostile environment that I muddled through daily. Was I not worthy to work at this historically black college? Did I not belong here? What did I have to do and what did I need to look like to earn the privilege of giving back to my institution and to students that look like me? These are some of the questions that I asked myself daily and I found myself converting back to my former self as I started planning my exit (Flight). Finally after I was tired of crying over it, I just got mad. Mad enough to decide that no one was going to run me away from my HBCU (Fight). Despite the negative undertone that was created, it is important to articulate that the majority of my colleagues were very supportive of me as a junior faculty member and we forged strong working relationships. Yet I still felt compelled to prove myself worthy to be there. So I worked and I worked hard to create a niche where I could utilize my talents. Because I was the only black woman in my department, the students naturally migrated to me and my advisee roster kept growing and growing. Suddenly I found myself with graduate students, many undergraduate trainees, and a long list of committee obligations. My office had a revolving door due to my open door policy for students. It became the counseling center, the cafeteria (students are always hungry), the prayer closet, the academic resource center, the complaint department, and a place to feel safe. Students were sending their friends from other departments to come see me for help. I didn't mind because it was my turn to pay it forward.

After my third year, I successfully applied for promotion to associate professor and was tenured two years later. I devoted so much of my time and energy to work that the first three years of my youngest child's life were a complete blur. When I realized that she was turning three and I couldn't recall the details of her second birthday, I was horrified. To this day, I don't know how my marriage survived, and there were several times that I was sure it was ending. Six years later, with tenure behind me, I was ready to relax and enjoy the good life of a college professor. As you can see, I was still very naïve.

## Stepping out of the Box

Going to work became very mundane and robotic. I still worked long hours, always had multiple projects going on, and remained involved with the students and student-centered activities. Unfortunately, I endured some hurtful situations as a result of academic politics that made me start thinking about the next stage of my life. I no longer wanted to be the "go-to girl" when there was some grunt work that needed to be done or when a black face was needed at student orientation. I had allowed other people to lock me in a box defining what position I was to play in the game. I was suffocating and needed a way out and I found it through Dr. Orlando Taylor and the NSF/OURS (Opportunities for Underrepresented Scholars) program. This new and innovative program designed to prepare women of color at HBCUs for academic leadership was exactly what I needed and, a year later, I had a new sense of self-confidence and an arsenal of knowledge to transition to the next level of academic leadership. The walls of the box that held me captive for eight years had been obliterated.

Over the next two years, I transitioned to several leadership positions and was promoted to full professor. Through these multiple transitions, my leadership style has evolved to become flexible and transitional. If I had to use one term to define my leadership style, it would be "authentic." My stories of my life, both personal and professional, have contributed to whom I have become and to my continuous evolution as a leader. Authentic leadership is truly being yourself while working to leave positive impressions on the lives of those you serve. Authentic leaders don't strive for perfection, but instead are committed to demonstrating excellence. Notably, authentic leaders are not afraid to show vulnerability by caring for the people they serve. This, combined with strong morals and self-awareness, clearly define who I am.

# My Life's Story

### Michel Reece, PhD

There is no defined or "expected" path for female leadership, especially in a STEM (science, technology, engineering and math) field. It is not an obvious option for young girls to become leaders because they rarely see one. As I considered my journey to becoming a STEM female leader, I realized, quite accidentally, that I wasn't supposed to be one. Throughout my childhood, teenage, and even young adulthood years, I was encouraged to take on supportive rather than leadership roles. I had a nice smile, a pleasant personality, and passable intelligence to make the male leader look good. Although there were obstacles, I still became a female STEM leader. Here is my story.

As I consider my life's journey from its beginnings to where I am today, I'm thankful to God for his provisions, protection, and peace. My life's story begins in Baltimore, Maryland where a young girl was raised by Jamaican immigrant parents. The youngest of five, I learned lessons about the importance of hard work, spiritual commitment to God, appreciation of family, respect for authority and, most of all, the value of education. From the time I could speak and read, my parents were always talking about us getting a good education, perhaps it was because they didn't receive more than high school and some college education themselves. I used to listen to these lessons, dreading the lectures about going to school or learning a trade.

Although my parents weren't college graduates, they acted as if they were. My father was an expert welder, often the foreman or supervisor on each job he held and my mother was a nursing technician, often training others and providing the best care to her patients. As I was growing up, I saw how my parents worked selflessly to provide a home, consistency, and love to five children. My siblings and I noticed that my parents' work ethic was so high that they rarely missed a work day or called in sick and were never late. What I saw in them growing up were those principles of honesty, integrity, and attention to detail that I still uphold today.

Growing up in Baltimore, it was not obvious that I had the option to become a leader, but there were major influences. My greatest female influence was my mother. She was the eldest of 13 children, very opinionated, passionate, thorough, quite verbal and had a "take charge" attitude. If something needed to be done, she would find a way to get it done. One could say that when my father wasn't around, she was definitely in charge. Others would say that when my father was around, she was still in charge. She wasn't disrespectful, but very industrious. She allowed my father to be the man in the home. I say "allowed" because it was clear that she chose and acquiesced to my father's authority in the home. It wasn't done "kicking and screaming," but with trust and love for her life partner. My father already knew that he needed her more than she needed him. She had an independent spirit about her. However, it was clear that the home was her domain; it was run like an industry. The kids were up each morning by a certain time, dressed, and taken to school. Chores were allocated; if work was not done satisfactorily, cuts were made—in allowances, entertainment, friend time, etc. My mom always told me never to depend on anyone to do my work for me; I must do it myself. Self-reliance has helped me out of serious situations many times. My mom was also selfless in her giving. She gave of her time, her resources, her home, and her family to help others in need. She could bark out orders one minute and serve you like royalty the next minute.

My mom was my first exposure to female leadership. Her domain of influence was the family, the home. But what about the outside world? What female roles were portrayed and frequently displayed by women? I consistently saw women portrayed as the housewife, the teacher, the administrative assistant, the associate who supports the CEO or VP, the mother, the facilitator—but rarely the director, the president, the CEO, the engineer, the innovator, the negotiator, or the manager.

As I progressed through my elementary and high school years, at every turn I tried to run away from any leadership roles or tasks. I thought it was too much responsibility for the headaches you have to endure in dealing with other people. I wasn't too successful at rejecting leadership roles because I was often the team lead in the lab group, president of this organization, or vice president of something else. I recall a time in my high school English class when we were discussing the book *Lord of the Flies*. This book was about a group of well-to-do boys who were stranded on a deserted island and began to fight each other for survival. My English teacher asked the class, "Who here do you think would survive on a desert island?" Everyone unanimously said it would be me.

Boy, was I surprised. Why me? you wonder. They felt that I would be the most resourceful. Who would have thought that? Surely not I. However, as I look back now, I realize that I was friendly with the smart kids, the popular kids, the sports kids, the eccentric kids, the theatrical kids, the unpopular kids, and even the bullies. I was a likeable person and I tried to be kind to all. However, I still ran away from anything distinctly leadership-like.

In college, I found my voice. I began my academic career as a freshman at Morgan State University in the Fall of 1991. Initially I was quiet, but as I progressed through my sophomore, junior, and finally my senior year, I got louder. In a degreed program such as engineering, where women are minorities, you have to speak up to get your point across. I usually tended not to speak, but when I am passionate about a subject matter or a person, you can't get me to shut up! Although it was not explicitly said, it was implied that the men were the highest performers in the engineering program. I remember correcting a particular professor numerous times regarding the pronunciation of my name. He always called me Michael, when I clearly and quite often told him my name is Michel. Also, I was the team lead again for quite a few lab groups, organizing and delegating tasks for others. As I reflect back, I realized even then that I was detail-oriented and wanted to make sure assignments were done to my standard, often motivating others not to settle for mediocrity, but to pursue excellence. I had a knack for recognizing others' strengths and weaknesses quickly and using that to assist with assignment completion. I wasn't an opportunist or someone who used information to hurt others; I just wanted to do the best job, because as a student that was my responsibility. I wasn't trying to be perfect, but I wanted to make a good impression each time, because anything with my name on it is a representation of who I am.

In my postgraduate and early professional career, I decided that I didn't want to be a leader. The headaches of relating to and dealing with people, their personalities, their quirks and attitudes were something I'd rather leave to someone else. I watched my pastor, my advisor, and my dean deal with some very difficult people who were often judgmental, unproductive, and unsupportive. It was too much work to be a leader! If leadership was just based upon one's skills and talents, then perhaps I would have had a better view of it; however, being an effective or transformative leader requires the unique skills of influencing others and relating to diverse populations who have different needs, experiences, characteristics, backgrounds, and beliefs that vary from your own. Even with this mindset, I was still engulfed in leadership roles—assistant director of a research group, spokesperson for graduate students who had issues with the administration, and team lead for research initiatives. After some time had passed, I began to realize: I cannot escape it any longer; I might as well embrace the idea of being a leader.

Now, as a tenured faculty member, I want to be a good leader, to be a role model for the students I mentor and advise. I cannot run away from leadership because it is a part of who I am as a person. I now realize it's more than it being just about me; it's more about effecting change to bring about positive outcomes not only for me, but also for those whom I serve and the organization in which I do serve. My previous academic experiences in leadership roles have helped me to value people, integrity, hard work, and the pursuit of excellence. I'm still passionate, especially about those things that impact my students and their outcomes. I believe that being an authentic leader requires passion. When others see that you are passionate, committed to what you do, not self-seeking, they are more willing to interact with you. I want to leave a legacy, one in which writers can say, "Dr. Reece stepped up to the challenge and made this a better place for me and my children after me."

# Back Seat Preference: Drive When Needed

Kimarie Engerman, PhD

## JOURNEY

*"Even when I am unaware, my words and actions impact a life."*
– Kimarie Engerman

As I look back on my life, I recognize that my mother has made a significant impact on the person I am today. My mother was the eldest of 13 children. She grew up in an era where older children had to drop out of school to help take care of their younger siblings. My grandparents told her that this would occur if she ever had to repeat a grade. At a young age, my mother understood the value of an education and vowed to obtain one. Unfortunately, my mother struggled with algebra in the ninth grade and had to repeat that grade. However, she did not inform her parents. On the first day of classes for the new school year at her Catholic school in the Virgin Islands when she returned home, my mother told her parents that there was only one space left in the 10th grade class and the nuns placed someone else in it. For some reason, her parents believed her and my mother was able to repeat the 9th grade and then continue to complete high school.

When I was growing up, my mother repeatedly told that story. She was extremely proud of her high school diploma. My mother worked at a school and at the start of the school year all employees would have to attend additional workshops if they did not have a high school diploma. My mother was allowed to leave early and was extremely happy that she had her high school diploma. I never realized until later in life the impact my mother's possession of a high school diploma had on me.

In the 11th grade, I vowed to obtain a doctoral degree because it was the highest degree possible in academia. Additionally, I wanted to become a professor at the University of the Virgin Islands. When I went to college, I participated in the Ronald E. McNair Post-Baccalaureate Achievement (McNair) Program, which was designed to prepare students for doctoral studies through research and scholarly activities. The McNair Program introduced me to writing research proposals, took me on graduate school visitations, and taught me how to apply to graduate school. More importantly, the McNair Program equipped me with all of the tools I needed to successfully obtain my doctoral degree.

Therefore, knowing my dream to become a college professor, one can imagine my excitement when my doctoral fellowship allowed me to participate in the Preparing Future Faculty program (PFF). I really could not believe a program such as PFF existed. PFF exposed me to the various issues involved in having a career in academia. My training in the art of college teaching today is highly reflected in my classroom style and student evaluations.

As a junior faculty, I participated in the Quality Education for Minorities Leadership Development Institute (LDI). The LDI was a year-long program for STEM (science, technology, engineering, and mathematics) junior faculty to enhance leadership and research capabilities. LDI allowed me to serve as a research scholar at the Spatial Intelligence and Learning Center at Temple University. Through participating in the LDI, I was able to be the principal investigator on my first grant from the National Science Foundation.

The leader I am today is a reflection of my mother. As a child, I internalized the fact that my mother went as far as she could in her time. Therefore, I needed to go as far as I could in my time. The sky is my limit. As such, I strive to be the best in all my endeavors. More importantly, I readily take advantage of opportunities for growth and development presented to me.

## LEADERSHIP PURPOSE

*"Purpose is fulfilled when you follow your heart."*
Kimarie Engerman

Because my mother's journey ended with her high school diploma, I had every right to be content with the fact that my dreams were accomplished when I obtained my PhD and became a Professor at UVI. I can honestly say that serving on a college campus was my life's calling. When I am in the classroom having a lively discussion with my students as they learn the concepts, I am in my element. I obtain great satisfaction from seeing the difference I have made in even one student's life. I love mentoring and helping students recognize and embrace their potential. Moreover, I have a deep calling to make a large impact on campus and in the Virgin Islands community as a whole. I want to be in a position that allows me to provide opportunities for advancement to students similarly to what I received as an undergraduate and graduate student. I want UVI students to be just as competitive for graduate school as students on the mainland. Even though I am at the same time building my scholarship, my joy is the fact that psychology students are given the opportunity to engage in research. Working as research assistants on my research projects has strengthened my students' applications for graduate school.

Although I absolutely love teaching, I found myself wanting to do more with my skills and abilities. I had a passion to become an academic leader able to provide more opportunities and create policies that benefit students. Knowing that there is no end to my journey, I recognized that in order to grow and not become complacent, I need to join the UVI administrative team. Coming from a background of participating in preparatory programs, however, I refused to do so without the proper training. For this reason, participating in the OURS Program was the next logical step in my career. Nonetheless, being an academic leader is not about placing a checkmark on my to-do list. Leadership is about service.

## LEADERSHIP STYLE

*"I embrace my leadership style. I do not have to be on the stage to be a leader. It is perfectly okay to lead from within the group. Leaders produce outcomes."* Kimarie Engerman

According to Mintzberg (1998), covert leadership is displayed when a group of highly qualified individuals works together on a project or task. I am a covert leader. I believe in being a part of the team and actively involved in the day-to-day activities. I engage in doing rather than leading. I love working with individuals that know what needs to be done and do it. The main advantage for my leadership style is that I tend to have the full cooperation of my subordinates. People enjoy working with me because I do not control their actions.

As a covert leader, I work best with professionals who require minimum supervision. Therefore, I prefer to give tasks without having to provide detailed instructions on how to complete the tasks. More importantly, the tasks are completed with a high degree of accuracy and professionalism. Also, there is no need for me to abuse power. I believe the individuals I work with should want to be a part of the team and will do their part to make the project a success. Consequently, there is no need for me to spend a significant amount of time empowering the group.

I am mindful that my leadership style preference does have disadvantages. Because I work with professionals, I have to be extremely sensitive when providing feedback. This is important to know because I cannot be overly critical. To avoid embarrassing the individuals on my team, negative feedback has to be given to the group and not the specific individual. Yet this can be problematic in that the individual who needs the feedback might think the feedback was not directed toward him/her and might continue with the same behavior.

Another disadvantage is that my covert leadership style is not effective for those individuals that focus on their personal success as opposed to the team's success. If individuals are pushing their personal agenda, the team's objectives will not be accomplished. Chaos and discontentment will occur. This creates a negative environment that is contrary to the collegiality I need to function effectively. For this reason, when leading, I have to obtain buy-in from everyone involved in order to make sure everyone is using the same agenda.

It is important that I have recognized and fully embraced my covert leadership style. I reminisce on a comment a good friend of mine made during our college years. We were home on break and were about to walk through a crowd at the club. I told my friend to lead the way and her response was that I needed to learn

44

to lead and not follow. I was taken aback by her comment because I never perceived myself to be a follower. I knew I was a leader, but my style was different than hers.

I understand now that some people are of the mindset that if you are not in the forefront, you are not a leader and also that some might believe leaders must always give input on a particular topic. Those beliefs are contrary to who I am as a person. I am not one to be onstage "spitting out fluff." I am not a talker; I am a worker. I prefer to work behind the scenes and accomplish the goal. More importantly, I believe a successful project is a reflection of the group. Unfortunately, my collectivist approach does not sit well with others. And the good news is that it is okay. I remember being chastised by a colleague after the successful implementation of a program I led. My colleague felt I should have accepted the accolades as opposed to sharing them with the team. I accepted the constructive criticism. Although I still believe in recognizing the team when the team's project is successful, I learned to personally accept accolades when I accomplish something. The reality is that I am a covert leader. Everyone leads differently, and it is a matter of recognizing one's style and using it to be effective.

## LEADERSHIP ROLES AND TRANSFORMATION

*"My gifts will make a room for me and bring me before great men."* Proverbs 18:16

*"A woman diligent in her business will stand before kings."* Proverbs 22:29

As a covert leader, I lead best from within the group, so it is not surprising that I have few leadership titles. I never volunteer for leadership positions. Some of the leadership roles I have held were not intentionally sought. I remember during my first year at the university, my chair asked if I would be interested in serving on a specific university-wide committee to plan an annual event. The committee membership was comprised of faculty and staff. At the first meeting, the committee members were extremely disgruntled. They were complaining about things that had occurred the year prior and no one wanted to serve as chair. After listening to the various exchanges with people talking of getting off the committee, in an attempt to obtain clarity, I asked what being chair entailed. That question resulted in the committee appointing me as chair. Immediately, everyone said they were willing to work with me and that is exactly what they did.

The event was a success for the five years that I served as chair. I believe it is credited to my covert leadership style in which I allowed committee members to take the lead in their respective area and contribute to the whole project. Each year, I wanted to relinquish my chair title, but the committee members refused to work with anyone else in that capacity but me. Eventually I had the provost intervene by appointing someone else to serve as chair. If I had not done so, today I might still have been the chair of that committee.

My role as principal investigator (PI) on a grant from the National Science Foundation is another example of a leadership position I did not seek. During one of our team meetings, my two co-principal investigators believed I was the ideal person to serve as PI. The thought of serving as PI did not cross my mind. I willingly accepted the position and I am thankful for the opportunity. Serving as PI opened the door to many other opportunities for advancement for me.

Unlike those two leadership roles mentioned, I actively sought the position as UVI Provost Fellow. Knowing that my career is in academia, I saw serving as Provost Fellow as an opportunity to facilitate my transition to higher education administration one day. I love working as a provost fellow. Half of my load is spent teaching, so I still get to interact with students. The other half is spent leading specific initiatives sponsored by the Provost Office. Although my projects keep me busy, I purposely created an additional objective. I felt when I left the position, I should possess a thorough understanding of what being a provost entails. Therefore, I asked to shadow the provost. I attend certain meetings and I am intricately involved in the inner workings of the office.

Now as I write this document, I have been selected to serve as Interim Dean for my college. I am extremely excited because this opportunity allows me to "test" the position to see if serving as dean is something I really want to do. The downside is that not everyone will be supportive because I have not been Program Coordinator or Department Chair. Email correspondences have already started circulating about the decision. Nevertheless, that is not my issue, not my battle to fight. My focus is on doing my best and making sure my name continues to be associated with "excellence." I will remain diligent in what I do and watch doors open for me. I will continue to be true to who I am in terms of my beliefs and values. A colleague accurately described me as a hard worker, honest, and fair. I am not going to change into something/ someone I am not because I have a leadership role.

Yet, as I claim my identity as an academic leader, I am thankful to the OURS Program for equipping me with tools needed to be successful. In my transformation, my outlook on my contribution to the university has changed. The focus is no longer on my individual contribution. Originally, I would challenge myself to answer the following questions each academic year: (1) What can I do to make the university a better place? and (2) How can I improve the university? As a leader, my focus is now on working with others to make sure the university's needs are met. This involves holding others accountable for the institution's mission, vision, and strategic goals. I have to engage in consensus building and empowering others. Additionally, I have to look at the big picture and make tough decisions that are in the best interest of the university. Therefore, it is key that I remember not to take things personally. The reality is that not everyone will be pleased with the decisions I make. However, if I remain honest and fair, although someone might not like my decisions, they have to respect them.

## AUTHENTIC LEADERSHIP

*"I can only give you the best if you allow me to be me."*
Kimarie Engerman

Authentic leadership means being true to who I am, letting the real me be exemplified when I lead. I will not be effective if I am modeling someone else's style. In being authentic, I need a sense of self-awareness. I know I am in my element when I am motivating and encouraging others. Also, I know that I value fairness, equality, and integrity. These traits I saw in my mother when she would go to great lengths to make sure all my cousins got a small gift for Christmas. These values are still with me. When I lead, I am very inclusive. I like people to be a part of the decision-making process.

I am intrinsically motivated. I experience satisfaction when I have made a difference in someone's life. Knowing that I have helped someone makes me experience joy. I do not like the limelight and would rather work behind the scenes. I am often described as being modest. As I said before, I am learning to graciously accept praise. I have been working on this and tend to bite my cheek when I am singled out for recognition. Moreover, I am not driven by money or external rewards. I tend to do things that I have a genuine interest in rather than those that merely offer benefits.

I can honestly say that my life is integrated. I am the same person in all aspects of my life. I am a peacemaker, an optimist, and a conservative. I love to encourage others to reach their full potential. Additionally, I love to laugh and I am full of energy. There is always laughter in my classroom and my undergraduate research assistants and I are always laughing.

As I climb the ladder, I can see that it is truly lonely on the top. Even though I value my support system, I rely heavily on my relationship with God. I start and end my day with prayer. God gives me strength, encourages me when I am weak, gives me peace when I am discomforted, and keeps me humble when I succeed. This relationship allows me to be an authentic leader. Because I accept who I am, I lead effectively.

## ADVICE TO ACADEMIC LEADERS

*"Following the advice I give will double my success."*
Kimarie Engerman

## Establish Balance

Maintaining work-life balance is critical to your success. Work-life balance is the ability to accomplish professional tasks and personal responsibilities without being stressed out on a daily basis. This requires managing your time, and not your energy. Having balance allows you to complete tasks at work as well as have time to spend with family or engaging in leisure activities. To obtain balance, it is beneficial to establish priorities and create a work schedule. Prioritization can be done through creating a ranking system based on the importance of tasks. The four quadrants of time-management system developed by Stephen Covey (Czartoryski, 2012) is then used to determine what is urgent, important, not urgent, and not important. A visual list will allow you to spend the time completing tasks that are important, but not urgent. It removes the anxiety of having to complete a task a few minutes before it is due.

Additionally, having a work schedule is necessary to help you stay on task. With a schedule in place, you can determine when certain tasks will be completed. A suggestion would be to use a daily planner broken into 15-, 30-, and 45-minute time slots. This allows activities to be adequately scheduled. More importantly, it is important that you stick to the schedule.

Also, others need to respect your schedule as well. Once regular changes are made and frequent disruptions are allowed, others will think it is okay to disregard your schedule. Your day will end with no productivity because you will be pulled in different directions. The bottom line is prioritization, and schedules create a cushion in your day to address emergencies which from time-to-time may occur.

## Say No

If the request does not feel right, say no. If the request is outside your scope of interest, say no. If the request requires more time than you have to give, say no. If the request requires working with individuals whose work ethics/work style is incompatible with yours, say no. If you just do not want to do it, say no. Some people have a difficult time saying no to requests. However, in order to maintain your sanity, you will have to say no at times. There is no need for you to commit to a task you fully well know you do not have the time or interest to fulfill. Saying no allows you to control your stress level. When you do say no, there is no need for a lengthy explanation. Be polite and keep it moving. An example of a response to give is, "I am sorry, but I am not available. I have other obligations that interfere with my ability to assist you. I do wish you well with this endeavor."

## Find a Sponsor

You probably already have mentors. However, once you know the distinction between a mentor and a sponsor, you will quickly realize that you need a sponsor as opposed to a mentor to help you advance. In an ideal world, you would have both. However, if given a choice, find a sponsor. A mentor is not actively involved in your career as a sponsor would (Ibarra, Carter, & Silva, 2010). Mentors are role models, they provide emotional support, give insights on how to navigate the academy, and will help you increase your sense of self-worth. On the other hand, sponsors hold senior positions and have influence. They will expose you to promising opportunities and make sure you are considered for positions that will enhance your skills. Also, sponsors will introduce you to individuals who may assist you in obtaining your career goals and mention your name when you are not present at senior level meetings. Sponsors will speak so highly of you and your qualifications that their colleagues will be seeking your services. Having a sponsor will help you feel as if you belong at the institution and that you have meaning in what you do. As I said, if you want to advance your career, find a sponsor.

I cannot close this section without bragging about my sponsor. I have a wonderful sponsor in my life. My sponsor is significantly responsible for my career achievements over the past six years. While I was still fairly new at my institution, she sought me out because she was aware of the work I did during my postdoc. She presented me with the opportunity to participate in the LDI that propelled my research agenda. Also, at the time, although my sponsor was the dean of a different college, she would include me on many research projects. Once she invited me to an NSF solicitation planning meeting, which resulted in my being the PI on a National Science Foundation grant and other grants. Moreover, when the OURS program was first funded, I found out about it through my sponsor. She willingly wrote my institution's nomination letter. Because of my sponsor, I have held many leadership positions on campus, the most recent positions being provost fellow and the upcoming position as interim dean. I am extremely thankful that I have someone in my life that knows my capabilities and recognizes my potential.

## Remember to Say Thank You

Do not forget your manners. My late Uncle Gravy's favorite saying was that manners will take you through the world. As a leader, your success is based on the contributions of others. Take the time to acknowledge them. You will be amazed at what a small thank you either verbally or electronically will do for your career.

# References

Czartoryski, A. (2012). The four quadrants of time management. Retrieved from http://czarto.com/2012/04/24/four-quadrants-of-time/

Ibarra, H., Carter, N. M., & Silva, C. (2011). Why men still get more promotions than women. *Harvard Business Review*, 80-85.

Mintzberg, H. (1998) Covert leadership: Notes on managing professionals. *Harvard Business Review*, 140-147.

# Becoming and Embracing a Transformational Leader: Strategies and Pitfalls at each Phase of a Leadership Journey

Amber Hodges, PhD

Recently, I earned a post-graduate certificate in Academic Leadership through the Opportunities for Underrepresented Scholars (OURS) Fellowship program. One of our first assignments was to complete an Everything DiSC® Work of Leaders Assessment to Action. This assessment classifies persons with one of four DiSC leadership personality styles: D – Dominance; i – Influence; C – Conscientiousness; and S – Steadiness. The profile identified me as an influencer or an "i" and some traits that describe me would include enthusiastic, outgoing, engaging, and spirited. I am expressive and comfortable in social settings. These personality traits have both positively and negatively impacted each phase of my leadership journey. My hope is that this essay provides aspiring leaders with strategies for advancement in leadership at various stages of development. Additionally, my aim is that the reader becomes aware of how their leadership personality style can impact their overall development into a leader as well as potential leadership opportunities.

# Leadership Phase One—Modeling Effective Leadership

The development of my leadership skills was unintentional, though I have held formal and informal leadership positions at each stage of my career. My leadership journey began during my college matriculation where I was able to excel in both coursework and co-curricular activities. In addition, I was an active student leader throughout my entire college career and held leadership positions ranging from secretary of the dorm council to high-level student government positions. There were two factors that impacted my leadership development at this early stage. First, I was able to observe upperclassman who were also women of color in leadership positions and model their leadership style while honing my own. Second, faculty advisors and administrators provided guidance in an encouraging and nonthreatening manner. Both factors provided me with a strong support system and allowed me to emerge as a campus leader in a safe and nurturing environment. These factors, coupled with my enthusiasm and communicative personality, allowed me to develop into and successfully become a campus leader. Because of these experiences I began to self-identify as a leader and my leadership style began to emerge. Through my various campus leadership positions, I learned that I could lead and influence others by helping them feel included and empowered. Though I was early in both my leadership journey and my career, I was able to glean valuable lessons from this phase. The first is, model effective leadership styles of strong leaders that resonate with you. Secondly, it is good to seek guidance and counsel from trusted advisors. Utilization of these key strategies influenced my development into a transformational leader. Transformational leaders are viewed as leaders who stimulate and inspire others, resulting in followers developing their own leadership capacity. This type of leader grows followers into leaders by responding to individual needs, empowering them, and aligning the objectives and goals of the individual followers, the leader, and the organization (Bass & Riggio, 2010). My leadership journey may not have been deliberate, but I have developed into an authentic transformational leader in higher education just the same.

## Leadership Phase 2—Pitfalls of an "i"

After college, I entered graduate school, primarily focused on performing well in my courses and conducting research in the lab. Once I arrived, I quickly realized that there were differences between me and the other students, with the first and most obvious being that I am a woman of color. However, I did not experience any overt negative interactions and received tangible support from faculty, resulting in my completing my coursework and my dissertation. I was able to navigate through my courses and worked productively in the lab. My "i" leadership personality made it easy to be outgoing and engage others; therefore I was well liked by my peers and was included in social outings. Therefore, though I was comfortable and well-liked, I unfortunately did not realize that I was not receiving vital professional development. For example, I completed my dissertation successfully, but was never taught how to convert the research studies into articles that could be published in peer-reviewed journals. Further, I was never encouraged to collaborate with other faculty members or colleagues while in graduate school or post-graduation. In particular, these missed opportunities stalled the development of my writing abilities, an essential skill needed by all scientists. Finally, there was no real discussion of next career steps, such as how to develop an eventual research program once I graduated or how to pursue a postdoc position.

At this point in my career, my limited professional development was partially due to my lack of awareness. Specifically, I did not have a good understanding of the specific leadership skills and development I needed to gain while in graduate school. This lack of awareness was coupled with the fact that I got along well with both faculty and peers. So while I was included and treated well by my colleagues, I was not being considered for opportunities that would enhance my career. Since my overall experience in the classroom and lab was positive, I did not understand that I was actually at a disadvantage by not receiving meaningful career guidance. Experiencing these disparities meant that I was not being groomed to be a leader in my field or for a career in higher education. Instead, I graduated as a proficient scientist with little appreciation of the skills I needed to move my career forward. I now understand that, though I was well liked, I was not well poised to advance my career in any meaningful way. Throughout graduate school, I made mistakes that stifled my career growth and misused my "i" traits. While it was nice to be well liked and easily engage with faculty and students, I should have been using these same skills to progress in the next steps of my career. I should have requested additional training and opportunities.

Despite not receiving some aspects of professional development, there were some positive advances in my leadership style. Particularly, I was gaining leadership skills in the areas of teaching and mentoring students that would serve me well later in my career. Though the culture of a research-intensive institution did not view these activities as important as those that focused on publishing and securing funding, I was able to discover some useful lessons and receive training that aided me as I advanced in my career. While conducting my dissertation research, I mentored undergraduate research assistants and guided them through graduate school preparation and other student projects. I displayed innate leadership characteristics with my guidance, and these students transitioned from students who just followed my directives into wonderful research assistants who had ownership over their work. My leadership style of providing feedback and showing them that their participation was important for the successful completion of the study, helped to empower them. Though unaware at the time, I was displaying transformational leadership as I inspired my followers to commit to a shared vision and goal. In addition, under my tutelage, these students became innovative problem solvers and developed into leaders in their own right. In the same way, I was able to share my research vision with my students, leading them to be vested in the research project. Also, during this time it would have been to my advantage to seek out faculty and peers to vest in my becoming a leader.

## Leadership Phase 3—Pitfalls Persist

I was hired as a postdoc at a minority-serving institution and I was excited to guide and mentor minority students as well as continue to develop as a scientist. In particular, I was impressed with the university's commitment to student teaching and development. Initially, I was very pleased to be in this environment and learned the relevant research techniques and skills needed to conduct experiments in the lab. However, I began to notice that

I was not maturing into an independent researcher as swiftly as I anticipated and instead was spending the majority of my time managing the experiments and the students. However, I was not being trained in the skills needed (how to successfully publish a research article and/or how to craft a grant proposal) or being exposed to enough professional development that would help advance my career. Subsequently, when I attended professional conferences, I realized that my peers who attended graduate school with me were more advanced in their careers. They were actively publishing, presenting at professional meetings, and had begun to secure research funding, while I had not.

Again, I mistakenly was not using my "i" personality traits to promote my career. My engaging personality and desire to mentor students, while noble, were not allowing me to gain the skills needed to develop as a leader. Again, I discovered that being well liked and even appreciated did not equate to career advancement. The difference is that this time I understood my shortcomings. This resulted in my grappling with negative feelings and no longer believing that I was as smart or qualified as my peers.

Despite the frustration I felt in my personal career development, I once again was able to continue to hone my leadership style and effectively empower my followers, which in this case were my students, to achieve the goals of the lab. Engaging students through mentorship of their research projects and their professional development allowed me to continue to develop my transformational leadership style. Increasingly, it was becoming apparent to me that I was truly skilled at leading students as well as developing and creating training mechanisms that empowered them to succeed.

# Leadership Phase 4—Shift in Mindset

Despite what I considered to be minimal research productivity, I was hired in a tenure track position at an institution with a heavy emphasis on undergraduate training. Now I finally had the freedom to do what I was passionate about: teach and mentor students. I also realized that in order to be awarded tenure and promotion, I would have to demonstrate research productivity. Therefore, I successfully used my "i" personality traits to secure a training position in a laboratory off campus, with a very productive researcher who had mentored me during an undergraduate summer research experience. This mentor made it clear at the onset that they were truly vested in improving both my research skills as well as the professional skills needed to facilitate career advancement. This type of mentoring helped me to distinguish between a research mentor and a sponsor. Sponsors have positions and power to advocate for unrecognized talent and make decisions regarding advancement to high-profile, critical positions (Ibarra, Carter, & Silva, 2010). Mentors may act as sponsors; however, their roles and positions are very different. Sponsors must be highly placed in an organization and have significant influence on decisions regarding advancement, while mentors can be at any level in the organization. Finally, the ability to mentor does not depend on position or power, and selection as a mentor is likely to be related to scientific or professional credibility and reputation (Travis, Doty, & Helitzer, 2013). Throughout my training, I had only had mentors solely based on alignment of scientific interests and potential future career aspirations. I had never considered that a mentor could attempt to intentionally advocate for me, resulting in career advancement as well as placing me in positions of high visibility. This was now happening on a regular basis.

Though exciting, this experience was also humbling, as I would be treated and trained as if I was a graduate student or postdoc, even though I was an assistant professor. However, I realized that if I wanted to move my career forward and ever be a leader in higher education, I had to be willing to be retrained. One of the most important lessons I gained from this experience is that it is never too late to correct a mistake and acquire the skills and training needed for career progression.

This shift in mentor and laboratory led to a shift in my attitude. Specifically, I was now taking full ownership and responsibility for my career. Now, to be clear, my new mentor was very demanding and the rigor required to work in this lab was much higher than I had ever experienced. There was a very high learning curve and a high level of proficiency required at all times. However, I was receiving critical feedback that helped me to improve as a scientist and eventual leader. I was provided with research skills and opportunities that boosted my identity as a leader and being treated as a colleague. These opportunities improved my confidence and allowed me to begin to understand what was needed to not just survive but to thrive in my field. This sponsorship resulted in my co-authoring six papers, which helped me to secure promotion and tenure.

This transition to this new lab environment forced me to reflect on why my career was stagnant. I realized that I had allowed myself to be trained to be a "doer" rather than a "thinker" and had not been trained to think or work in an independent manner. I was taught to conduct scientific research, but not to advance my career. More importantly, I had to consider the reasons why I had not been trained or even viewed as a leader.

The first lesson I discerned after reflecting on my previous experiences was that being treated nicely is not the same as being trained as a leader in my field and ultimately in higher education. I had been naive in expecting that if someone had the title of mentor they would do everything in their power to teach me the skills I needed to advance in all areas. And while I was being trained as a scientist, none of my previous mentors ever saw me as a leader or assumed the role as sponsor. Therefore, training that would have facilitated my career advancement did not occur. However, I committed one huge mistake and that was not requesting to be considered for the same opportunities as my peers. Requesting opportunities may have caused my mentors to (1) realize that I was interested in being trained, and (2) begin to consider me as an emerging leader in my field who wanted to be challenged. Being silent was a major error on my part. Now, as a leader, when I see a beneficial opportunity that is not being offered to me, I request to be included. Sometimes, it is just a matter of making it known that I am interested in being considered.

## Leadership Phase 5—A Leader Emerges

During my third year as an assistant professor, I was accepted into the first cohort of the Leadership Development Institute (LDI), which was led by the Quality for Education for Minorities Network and funded by the National Science Foundation. This year-long program targeted junior faculty and was the first time I actively pursued formal leadership training. I received intensive professional development and my eyes were opened to information that my more successful colleagues had known for years. The most important lesson I learned from this program was to take full control over my research, teaching, and service activities and ensure that they benefited my career. I started to intentionally focus my efforts towards activities that would promote my career. I was more selective about the university service I performed and actively sought out professional service opportunities. Before LDI, I did not have a real understanding of the importance of professional service and, more importantly, I was not aware of how the networking involved in these opportunities would positively impact my career. This was the first time that I gained an understanding of factors beyond my research productivity that were important for my development as a leader in higher education. I also gained a much better sense of what type of training and professional development I lacked up to this point. A transformation began to take place during LDI and I began to self-identify as a leader within my department and at my university.

A second professional development opportunity that helped solidify my leadership style and my place as a leader was the OURS program. This year-long program was designed for women faculty at minority-serving institutions who aim to pursue high-level administrative positions in higher education. The most important lesson I learned being an OURS fellow was how to become an authentic leader. I learned it is imperative for me to pursue my passion while maintaining and displaying my core values of respect, integrity, and excellence. I have found that as I become an authentic leader, it is imperative that I remain self-aware. The first step in my self-awareness was acknowledging that though I am trained as a neuroscientist, I actually wanted to investigate research questions within the field of educational psychology. Admittedly, it took me several years to begin a new research program while actively developing and implementing mentoring structures for students of color in higher education. However, I have now achieved both.

Additionally, pursuing my passion required that I obtain professional development and training in a new subfield. Most importantly, it meant a change in my perspective, requiring that instead of only pursuing conventional measures of success (i.e., bench work, publications, grants to support lab work), I would instead measure my success in the positive impact my work has on my followers: the students. However, I have found that as I engage in authentic leadership, I enjoy my work, even though it can be challenging. I experience flow (Barsh & Cranston, 2011) and as a result, I have increased energy, and the students I am leading have aligned their vision with mine; they are empowered and becoming leaders in their own right. This satisfies me on both a personal and professional level and drives me to continue to both pursue my passion and embrace additional leadership roles. I have already developed and implemented several campus-wide mentoring structures for high-achieving STEM (science, technology, engineering, and mathematics) majors and my expertise is now being recognized and valued by various units within the campus community. I also seek out and receive more opportunities for professional service, which provides increased visibility outside of my campus in my professional field. I am now very cognizant of showcasing my expertise and leadership skills, as I have emerged as an authentic leader.

As I continue my leadership journey, I now utilize my "i" characteristics to benefit my career. I continue to identify leaders whom I can emulate and look for sponsors. I have become skilled at communicating my vision and growing my followers by aligning their goals with mine. Specifically, I have learned to engage others and allow them to share in my enthusiasm.

My advice to aspiring leaders is as follows:

1. Identify, learn, and embrace your leadership style

2. Identify, request, and seek out leadership opportunities to stretch you and help you grow and gain exposure

3. Communicate your vision clearly so that others align with you and your vision to move your career forward

4. Enthuse, engage, and empower your followers; and

5. Most important, don't rely on others. Create your own opportunities and be responsible for *all* aspects of your career.

# References

Barsh, J., & Cranston, S. (2011). Experience of flow. *How remarkable women lead: The breakthrough model for work and life* (pp. 261-269). New York: Crown Business.

Bass, B. M., & Riggio, R.E. (2010). The transformational model of leadership. In G. R Hickman, *Leading organizations: perspectives for a new era* (2nd ed.), pp. 76-86. Thousand Oaks, CA: SAGE Publications.

Ibarra, H., Carter, N. M., & Silva, C. (2010). Why men still get more promotions than women. *Harvard Business Review, 88*(9), 80-85.

Travis, E. L., Doty, L., & Helitzer, D. L. (2013). Sponsorship: a path to the academic medicine C-suite for women faculty? *Academic Medicine*, *88*(10), 1414-1417.

# Accidental Leader

Olga Bolden-Tiller, PhD

I was no Stephen Curry and would undoubtedly never be mistaken for an MVP on the basketball court, but my contributions definitely led to not one, but two state championship wins by the Pantherettes of Clinch County High. I remember in a radio interview during the playoffs of basketball season during my senior year of high school, just before one of the championship games, Mr. Elroy asking me how I fit in as starter (God knows I only averaged about four points a game, although I rocked in the assists department). I always remember replying that "I am the coach on the court." Low self-esteem has never been a major issue for me. And as I thought about my answer, I felt very confident in it. It was not the point guard who called most plays when we were on offense, but instead our coach most often looked to me to confirm our plays. I generally called out the plays for my teammates, making sure that we were in place to get things done. And even after this experience, I never really considered myself a leader per se, but looked to my role as the coach on the court as my contribution to the team. (Did I mention that I was not very fast either, and that it did not hurt to have a superstar on my team who later became a member of the WNBA?) Nonetheless, I was very clear in my role on that team and loved it greatly!

# Pathway to Leadership

Over the years, I never envisioned myself as a leader. I definitely have opinions about things. As a scientist, my mind seemingly almost automatically evaluates situations and when they are not moving forward, the pieces start to sort to a workable solution. This is a gift of puzzling that I knew I had, but never striven to apply as a leader, although I often have found myself in leadership roles either informally or formally.

For instance, while in graduate school, I was actively involved in the departmental graduate student association and served as an officer for several years. During my final year, I was recognized as Outstanding Graduate Student. Under my leadership, our departmental graduate student association began catering for organizations as a lucrative fundraiser that I am happy to say continues to this day. The funds from these activities led to numerous professional development opportunities for the graduate students within our department. As I completed my program and shared with my committee my plans to one day become a faculty member at an HBCU, I recall one of my committee members who is renowned in our field saying, "Call me when you become dean." I recall laughing it off, as I never intended to serve in a leadership role, but was eager to complete my postdoctoral training so that I could begin my own research lab as a faculty member.

Following graduate school, I transitioned into a postdoctoral position in a lab with several other postdocs and research assistants/associations. I enjoyed my experience and was happy to work on numerous projects beyond my own while in the lab. As the new kid on the block, I was happy to follow the lead of those in the lab, as we all had a great working relationship. It was not until a few months later that I realized that several of them had begun to see me as a leader in the lab, looking to me for advice on projects and beyond. This realization was revealed to me during the annual spring cleanup, of all things. I remember being approached by the senior postdoc in the lab with a question about how we should organize items in the lab. It is rare that I am at a loss for ideas, thus also rare that I am at a loss for words. In the months prior to the annual lab cleanup, I had made a few suggestions here and there based on my previous experiences and training, including a workshop that I had organized as a part of one of my professional societies, which focused on setting up a new lab. Apparently, the group had been pleased with some of my previous suggestions, which led to the request for additional inputs. I really found it interesting that the "veterans" were looking to me for guidance, but even at that time, I didn't necessarily see myself a "leader," but instead as a contributor to the group.

Since my first year as a graduate student, I was actively involved in the Society for the Study of Reproduction as a trainee. I really enjoyed the organization and its commitment to training young scientists. I was always eager to participate in the trainee activities, which afforded me many opportunities in professional development as a young scientist. During my second year as a postdoc, I decided to run for the position of trainee representative to the organization's board of directors. In that role, I had the opportunity to work with some of the top scientists in my field, not only as scientists, but as partners conducting the business of the organization. And it was during and subsequent to this period that I realized that my inputs were viewed as more than just contributions, but specifically sought from a leadership perspective. My accomplishments, including the establishment of a new award for the organization, and the accolades that I received for my contributions and accomplishments, contributed to my acceptance of leadership roles that were to come.

## A Woman Called to Lead

Only six months after beginning at Tuskegee University (TU), I was asked to serve as the program coordinator for the animal and poultry sciences program, which I was happy to accept. The potential of the program was so evident and I looked forward the challenges of providing eager and excited students the opportunities to realize their career goals. This was a project to me, really, not a call to leadership, not in my eyes. I like processing information and I am used to receiving it, sorting it and molding it into something useful . . . a project. Thus, I was able to tackle the challenges plaguing the program as such and was very excited about the results. I still considered what I did a part of a group effort, the group being the Animal and Poultry Sciences faculty, and indeed I was. But even then and with every leadership opportunity that I accepted thereafter, I recalled my old committee member saying "Call me when you become dean." And every year when I would see him at professional meetings, he still asks, "Are you dean yet?"

A few short years later, when I was asked to serve as the Assistant Department Head, again I looked on this in much the same manner; it reminded me of my high school basketball days, working with a very talented group of people to get a job done. In truth, it was not until I was asked to serve as the department chair that I really felt that I was being asked to *lead* folks. By that time, I had had the fortune of taking part in institutional projects that spanned the campus through the Preparing Critical Faculty for the Future program and had established relationships with others in positions of leadership or who were involved or desired to be involved in major change at their institutions, which had led me over time to ponder and to some degree implement improvements and ways to address challenges at my institution. In my new role as chair, for the first time I felt a sense of responsibility to lead a group of people and to ensure their success at their roles and subsequently that of the department as a whole. I remember actually asking my dean if there was some leadership training available to assist me in my new role and, although his answer was affirmative and he was supportive, that particular training was not available for almost another year. I did subsequently go on to pursue that training, but before it could even begin the Opportunities for Underrepresented Scholars (OURS) program was announced. I quickly pounced on that opportunity, so fast indeed that it was not until several weeks later that I realized I had actually signed up for a year-long program . . . a fact that many of my colleagues from the cohort still chuckle about often.

To a new appointee to an administrative position, the announcement of the OURS program was more than timely. From the start, it was clear that the tools OURS afforded me were of extreme value, resulting in the development of leadership skills that have come in handy again and again, resulting in positive impacts within my department and across my university. Of most value undoubtedly was the opportunity to view issues differently. As a faculty member, it is easy to view the game as a player; however, the OURS program gave me skills and insights that resulted in my viewing the game as a coach, giving me a greater perspective on the academy and how to implement advances in the academy.

For instance, during the first residency of the program, we were challenged to look at issues affecting our institutions, not from our positions as faculty members or our departments, but further. In addition to looking at the issues, we were to identify solutions that would work specifically for our individual institutions. The OURS program was essential in helping me look beyond my discipline to find resources to address said issues and, by bringing me together with a group of women from different perspectives, disciplines, and institutions, I was able to grow tremendously with regard to how I not only viewed issues, but how I moved to resolve issues. It is for this especially that I will be eternally grateful for the program. Further, the network that I have established through my involvement with OURS has been a blessing. Sharing in the triumphs of 19 other women continuously puts a smile on my face and keeps me centered. I know that I am not alone in this fight and that my efforts are not solitary nor are they in vain, as our collective efforts continue to have positive impacts at our institutions and subsequently on higher education as a collective.

And although the other training program was of benefit, it is sure that by far, OURS had the greatest impact on me—as a scholar, as a woman, and as a leader at an HBCU. Since completing the OURS program, I have been promoted to the role of assistant dean at my college and, just the other day when at a speaking engagement I ran into my old committee member who again asked, "Are you dean yet?" I was happy to share that I had gotten a step closer. I could see the smugness in his smile, but it filled me with joy knowing that, all those years ago, he saw something in me that I had not seen in myself. I am proud to know that I have nurtured the seed that was planted so many years ago. I mentally thank the directors of my youth ministry program for making me learn parliamentarian procedures when I was in grade school even though I did not want to. I thank my basketball coach for using my talents that I did not think were overly valuable and instilling in me and my teammates that "You've got to want it to win it." I thank my high school science teacher for encouraging my interest in physiology and my mother who was also a teacher and club advisor, for encouraging not only me, but hundreds of other students during her 38 years as an educator to excel and have fun as a member of the Future Homemakers of America (now Family, Career and Community Leaders of America). It is through these and numerous other opportunities that now come to mind that I have been given a sound foundation and the confidence to take advantage of opportunities, including the leadership roles that I have held, but also training such as that provided by OURS.

Too often we think of being called to serve women in particular, but OURS ensured that I had the tools to be not only a servant, but also a leader. I enthusiastically embrace my role as a servant-leader. This is term often coined by the late George Washington Carver, who has been quoted as saying "It is not the style of clothes one wears, neither the kind of automobile on drives, nor the amount of money one has in the bank that counts. These mean nothing. It is simple service that measures success." Carver was by far one of the most prominently known servant-leaders of his time, contributing much as a scientist and beyond to many, but looked upon as a leader. Thus, I am sure that it is no accident that I landed at Tuskegee University and that I have been identified as a person to provide a service to the institution in my current role, as I indeed share this philosophy wholeheartedly. So, to women

I say, "Listen to the voices in your head, the writings in the sand, or the whispers of the wind as they call you to lead, as in truth, it is another form of service, probably the most important!"

# A Persistent Path to Authentic Leadership

Jumoke Oluwakemi Ladeji-Osias, PhD

The earliest event that shaped my leadership journey occurred when I was in the 11th grade, at Federal Government Girls' College Abuloma—an all-girls boarding school in Southeastern Nigeria. At my school, the 12th grade girls held leadership positions, and were called prefects. The prefects were the school's student leaders, responsible for running the school once the faculty finished instruction in the afternoon and went to their homes off-campus. Prefects ensured that the boarders, about 95% of students, followed the daily schedule. These student leaders were also responsible for order in the dormitories after the teachers left for the day, and could punish students who did not follow the rules. Teachers and administrators chose the well-respected prefects. Both my teachers and the administrators told me that I would most likely be selected to become the library prefect in my 12th grade year. On the day of the announcement, I wore my best uniform, ready to walk up on the stage to assume my prefect role. Unfortunately, I was not chosen for any position, although many of my good friends were. That day, initially filled with anticipation of good news, quickly became the most disappointing day of my life. After recovering from my initial hurt, I held my head up high and came away with two lessons. The first was that until the "winner" is announced, do not get too excited. The second lesson was to be confident in myself and be proud of my achievements, even when I do not receive external validation or recognition. These lessons remain part of my core principles 25 years later.

According to George, Sims, Mclean, and Mayer (2007), "no one can be authentic by trying to imitate someone." Authentic leaders "know who they are." They are driven by passion and values, have strong relationships, commit to self-development, and are self-disciplined. The resulting emotional and intellectual decision-making produce superior results in the long term. To become an authentic leader, one must reflect on experiences that have been highly impactful, assess one's values and sources of motivation, and develop a plan to create an integrated, authentic life. Authentic leadership, for me, means that I stay true to who I am, highlighting my strengths and compensating for my weaknesses. At work, that means using my propensity for strategy and structure to ensure followership while also ensuring that I delegate to encourage task completion. Authentic leadership means that I have a personal culture that merges the rich African American heritage of my mother and the traditional Yoruba (Nigerian) heritage of my father. I value the transformational power of education, the importance of village and community in achieving progress, and remember the sacrifices made on two continents to ensure success for people of color. I promote engineering as an opportunity to demonstrate creativity and passion, and as a driver of innovation. Authentic leadership for me also means that even though it is not the culture at my institution, I must encourage others to take on leadership roles by setting term limits for myself.

Currently, I am an associate professor of electrical and computer engineering at Morgan State University (Morgan), an historically black college/university (HBCU) located in a residential area of Baltimore City. I have been on the faculty since 2001. The first department leadership role I held as a faculty member was to lead the assessment committee for our 2007 ABET accreditation visit. I was responsible for designing the assessment and evaluation framework, collecting all syllabi and assessment data from faculty, and contributing to the department's self-study. In that role, I learned how to lead faculty towards an important goal. The department chair was demanding and detail-oriented, which was a good learning experience for me, as the quality of my work improved. My performance in this role resulted in my being asked to take on more responsibility within the department. I was nominated to become the graduate coordinator for the department and was later promoted to associate chair. As the associate chair, I was responsible for leading the graduate program including student selection for the master's and doctoral program, advising and scheduling courses. I also oversaw the process of obtaining faculty input for departmental policies and curricular changes. I was not given any formal training for this position; instead, I participated in external professional development opportunities for women of color in engineering or women's studies at HBCUs, such as the Preparing Critical Faculty of the Future (PCFF) (American Assoication of Colleges and Universities, 2012) and Opportunities for UnderRepresented Scholars (OURS) (The Chicago School of Professional Psychology, 2016). Those programs were instrumental in providing me with a deeper understanding of the many facets of leadership and the expectations of administrators in higher education (Gardner, 2007; Sciame-Giesecke, 2008). They also provided access to an invaluable professional network that continues to contribute to my career success.

When I assumed the position of graduate coordinator, the electrical engineering graduate program was facing declining enrollment. My vision for the program was to increase the number of students and provide additional financial support to full-time students using extramural funding. To increase enrollment, I seized on an opportunity to develop a new master's of science program with concentrations in communications, signal intelligence, and power and energy systems that would be attractive to new students. This program has since outpaced enrollment in the existing master's of engineering program. Another step was to seek funding from the National Science Foundation (NSF) through the Scholarships in Science, Technology, Engineering and Mathematics program to provide scholarships to master's and doctoral students. Over a three-year period, I submitted two grant proposals, each of which was funded on the first attempt. The first one was designed to provide scholarships to undergraduate and master's students from four engineering departments in a unique peer mentoring program. The first scholarship program lasted five years and graduated about 30 undergraduates and 20 master's students. The second NSF funded grant is ongoing, provides scholarships for doctoral students, and has supported about 15 students.

With the student funding in place, my next focus was on building departmental capacity to compete for basic research funding. After three submission attempts, the department was awarded a grant from the NSF Centers of Research Excellence in Science and Technology (CREST) program through the Historically Black Colleges and Universities Research Infrastructure for Science and Engineering (HBCU-RISE). Having to revise our proposal twice provided opportunities for the department faculty to assess our areas of strength, to select the best leaders for the project, and to identify the faculty team that could support the HBCU-RISE project objectives. Accepting that a shared leadership model with a more senior faculty member as principal investigator created the best team was as a result of my strategic outlook.

After eight years in the position, I opted to step down as Associate Chair for Graduate Studies to provide leadership opportunities to others in the department and focus on new research opportunities. Although, the associate chair position did not have any associated funding or administrative support it gave me significant visibility at Morgan and allowed me to develop skills that can be translated to research and other leadership positions. The associate chair position has also given me significant confidence in my leadership skills. I have had to advocate for administrative support, introduce new degree programs, pursue extramural funding, and push for new faculty. More broadly, the faculty position at Morgan has also afforded me the opportunity to pursue my passion in creating opportunities for school K–12 youth to engage in engineering activities. I have partnered with Baltimore County (Maryland) 4-H to found a FIRST (FIRST, 2016) robotics program for elementary and middle school youth. The program has grown since 2013 to include participating in regional and state-wide FIRST competitions and enriching the local community though robotics demonstrations and workshops. This and other similar volunteer efforts provided the necessary background to create a Maker program for middle school boys in Northeast Baltimore supported by the Verizon Foundation. The Minority Male Maker program was launched in the summer of 2015 and, in nine months, introduced over 70 boys to 3D modeling and mobile application development for Android devices. This program received national coverage and continues to grow in scope (Bailey, 2015; Nadworny, 2015). The skills to design and implement such a high-visibility program were developed through PCFF and OURS.

One of my core values is that all people should be treated fairly and afforded similar opportunities. Leadership provides me with an opportunity to address injustices in society, particularly around education. My undergraduate degree is from the University of Maryland College Park and my graduate degree is from Rutgers, the State University of New Jersey. I had very limited knowledge about HBCUs before I started working at Morgan, except for memories of Howard University from my mother, an alumna. Since I have been at Morgan, I have come to appreciate the differences in the K–12 educational system and their impact on one's college choices. Many students at my institution come from school districts that do not prepare them for engineering careers. They come to us with limited calculus exposure because these advanced courses are not available at their high school, unless they are in schools targeted at gifted students. I am also distinctly aware of resource constraints in my department but have not let that limit my impact. Thus, I focused my extramural funding efforts on initiatives that can provide additional resources for Morgan students and faculty. I also developed programs for the youth who will one day become my students. These efforts have been fueled by my desire to ensure that minority students have access to facilities that are on par with students at other academic institutions.

# References

American Assoication of Colleges and Universities. (2012). Preparing Critical Faculty for the Future (PCFF). Retrieved

January 15, 2016, from https://www.aacu.org/pcff.

Bailey, L. F. (2015). New Program Introduces Young Black Men to Technology. Retrieved March 21, 2016, from http://www.huffingtonpost.com/linnie-frank-bailey/new-program-introduces-yo_b_7962636.html.

FIRST. (2016). K-12 programs for kids. Retrieved March 21, 2016, from http://www.firstinspires.org/.

Gardner, J. W. (2007). *The tasks of leadership. Project Kaleidescope Volume IV: What works, what matters, what lasts.* Retrieved from http://www.pkal.org/documents/Gardner_The-tasks-of-leadership.pdf.

George, B., Sims, P., Mclean, A. N., & Mayer, D. (2007). Discovering your authentic leadership. *Harvard Business Review*, (February), 1-8.

Nadworny, E. (2015). Coding Camp to Baltimore Schools: Bring Us Your Bored! Retrieved March 21, 2016, from http://www.npr.org/sections/ed/2015/08/01/427416157/coding-camp-to-baltimore-schools-bring-us-your-bored.

Sciame-Giesecke, S. M. (2008). *Non-positional faculty leadership. Project Kaleidescope Volume IV: What works, what matters, what lasts.* Retrieved from http://www.pkal.org/documents/Non-Positional Faculty Leadership—Sciame-Giesecke.pdf.

The Chicago School of Professional Psychology. (2016). NSF/OURS Program. Retrieved March 21, 2016, from http://www.thechicagoschool.edu/nsfours-program.

# Beyond Binary

Tamara Rogers, PhD

A family friend told me when I was deciding about college majors, "The problem is that you cannot decide whether you want to be your mother or your father." Even though no one asked me to choose, I was operating under a false sense of pressure to do so. The same holds true when addressing leadership opportunities. For me, embracing leadership opportunities has often seemed to be a tradeoff between choosing the leading to help get the job done and having to promote myself to be able to get to that position—leading versus the leadership title and self-promotion. Although I don't aspire to leadership for the sake of being a leader, I recognize that in various situations I may have contributions that can help. When I hold these back, it may actually delay the progress of the overall group. Authentic leadership for me is helping a team reach its goals while maintaining my personal integrity and respect for others. I enjoy helping others recognize and realize their potential.

## My First Leaders

My mother is a great example of using individual skills for the benefit of the group. As the technical person in the family, she experienced a middle management layoff that was a major career setback. During this time, she volunteered her time to help start a credit union. Although she had some management experience, her training was in electrical engineering. In the 20 years since that time, she has subsequently learned the relevant rules and regulations, managed and served as the CEO of the credit union, and served in the leadership of national credit union organizations. While this is her story, it is relevant to me for several reasons. I see her as an example of a person who is often tapped into leadership from among her colleagues and other leaders. She is tapped because others observe her competence and willingness to work and expect her to be effective. As that also happens to me, I am learning to overcome my initial inclination to avoid standing out, to avoid appearing as one who is trying to be "over" people. In addition to being recognized for her hard work and leadership skills, my mother accepts these responsibilities with grace, not a domineering spirit. These contribute to the understanding that one can lead effectively without demanding the title or any false sense of respect.

From my father I learned about the interpersonal side of leadership and harnessing power. Although he has a big physical presence, he often deals with people with a quiet power, wisdom, and humor. I find myself quoting some of his maxims, although I don't have strong memories of the specific incidents when he said them. Something about the way that they have stuck with me over time supports the idea of simple goals or objectives that can direct efforts. Words that serve to empower people are important and can be lasting. In addition, my father has training in nonviolent crisis intervention and can sometimes disarm a situation by not flexing the muscle he clearly possesses. I also embrace those things in myself. As I have gotten older, I have a greater appreciation for the strengths of my parents.

## It's a Matter of Style

In addition to the examples of leaders that I have experienced, formal study has helped me begin to see the wider array of leadership styles. For example, Eagly and Carli (2007) contrast democratic and autocratic leadership styles. The democratic style, also considered participatory, tends to be collaborative and gives participants a voice in decision making. The autocratic style, also considered directive, tends to make decisions without input from participants. My personal leadership style feeds from observing other leaders and my personal tendencies. I am able to describe it as tending toward the stereotype of women leaders being more collaborative and inclusive. For example, when leading or facilitating a discussion, I actively seek input from others. I may notice if there are people who have voiced no input or seem to have something to say based on their body language or expression and invite them into the conversation. Sometimes in committee work or breakout groups, I may add this collaborative component, especially if no leader specifically exists. This natural tendency to "pick up the reins" in those situations contrasts with my typical reluctance to jump into leadership opportunities. Being called the leader may be more of a hindrance than the actual doing of the task. I sometimes describe this as leading from behind or from the side.

I do recognize, however, that there are times that a leader has to make decisions that are not democratic or may not be popular. When working with students, I tend to begin with a democratic approach. When I am dealing with classroom issues or advising, I may state the objective and seek student input. It is often the case that they have reasonable solutions. They should participate in the decisions that affect them when it is something negotiable. There are times, however, when I "pull rank" and let them know that I am making the decision, even if it is not with the consensus, because it is what I deem to be the best and what I am willing to stand behind. McRae (1998) discussed the idea of determining the appropriate muscle level to adopt when negotiating with or influencing others. Given the choice, I would prefer the soft answer versus the maxim screamed from the rooftop.

I experienced a situation professionally that demonstrated using appropriate muscle level. A step in my career was in the hands of someone who was not being straightforward with me. A leader higher in the hierarchy intervened by bringing the situation to my attention, giving me alternatives, and allowing me to stand up and address the situation. What has stayed with me in this situation is a sense of there being sponsors, mentors, and advocates who may be involved in my career without my knowledge. I was also struck by the fact that this person did not want to begin by stepping in and asserting their power before allowing the chain of authority to work. I have since learned that the true authority of a leader defined by the role is called legitimate power (Raven, 2008). I have actually had the opportunity to utilize this tactic myself. There was a situation in which I was going to need to make and assert a final decision. I began, however, with low muscle level, thereby allowing the other person to come to the conclusion that we each deemed appropriate. The result is that I was able to assure that outcome without having to appear to fight for that outcome. Again, the individual was empowered instead of overpowered. Although I don't desire to be authoritarian, failure to be more directive may also unintentionally lead me to underestimate this part of my responsibility.

## It's Not One or the Other

Leadership does not require a person to choose one solution for every situation. Such an approach would most likely lead to discontent. I am learning that there is a power and energy that can come from embracing your strengths instead of running from them. The success of guiding by the example of hard work, listening to input, and leading with a low muscle level was presented in my earliest leaders. Learning about the contributions of academic leaders has helped me become more aware of different leadership styles. I am becoming better at assessing my capabilities and can humbly accept the responsibilities that fit. I have to consider the interests of the group rather than focus on any anxiety or apprehension that may arise. More important to developing authentic leadership is the ability to acknowledge the strengths I do have in order to identify and cultivate leadership styles that work for me and my values. I am far more comfortable with leading when I focus on the goal and refuse to be distracted by my own self-consciousness.

## References

Eagly, A. H., & Carli, L. L. (2007). *Through the labyrinth: The truth about how women become leaders*. Boston, MA: Harvard Business School Press.

McRae, B. (1998). *Negotiating and influencing skills: The art of creating and claiming value*. Thousand Oaks, CA: Sage Publications.

Raven, B. H. (2008). The bases of power and the power/interaction model of interpersonal influence. *Analyses of Social Issues & Public Policy, 8*(1), 1-22. doi: 10.1111/j.1530-2415.2008.00159.x

# Authentic Leadership From a Life's Story

Gloria Thomas, PhD

In the early 2000s, a call for authentic leadership arose. While this concept had been described briefly in earlier social science literature, a renewed focus on this theory studied leadership that is driven by an individual's core values, identity, and self-awareness (Gardner, Cogliser, Davis, & Dickens, 2011). This newer construct asserts that authentic leaders are motivated by a balance of extrinsic rewards and self-driven passion that is rooted in their own personal identity, which is consistent across all aspects of their lives. Some theorists further present the concept that the most effective authentic leaders are shaped, and constantly re-shaped, by their life story. Their inspiration comes from both positive experiences as well as negative experiences, such as great tragedy or adversity, that can be reframed into meaningful lessons and opportunities for growth during challenges, allowing an effective leader to emerge.

My own life story and journey to leadership are filled with the pursuit of authenticity. The beginning of my story is tremendously shaped by my upbringing as an "Army brat." I was born in an Army hospital at Fort Huachuca, Arizona and spent my childhood traveling the world with my father, who was a single parent. By the time I was in the 5th grade, I had lived in four different countries. Whether by nature, nurture, or pure survival, I learned to adapt to a variety of different environments. This includes an ability to mimic customs, behaviors, languages, and accents, sometimes without my even being aware of it. I have found that this skillset allows me to feel quite comfortable in a wide range of environments, including the boardroom, a live TV broadcast, the machine shop of a chemical plant, or the bank of a fish pond— one of my favorite places. While this early acquired ability has served me well, it has also intensified my pursuit of authenticity, although perhaps not until later in life.

Some of the early chapters of my life story include childhood experiences of rejection that were felt growing up as a half-African American, half-Asian American child in an economically depressed and predominately African American neighborhood (when I did live stateside). I endured taunting and teasing about being half-Chinese from many neighborhood bullies, which led to a heightened sense of self-awareness that can be a detriment, but also an advantage. However, my father's stern lectures on never backing down and my family's nurturing love for me also taught me to develop a thick skin and to rise to a challenge. Guided by those memories, I am determined never to isolate others because of differences, to ignore the naysayers, and to always see the value in varying walks of life and backgrounds. These experiences continue to shape my responses when under pressure as a leader, but also remind me that everyone has worth, value, and something to contribute.

Those chapters also ring loud with my father's many lessons. As a true "daddy's girl," I spent a great deal of time with my father, who enjoyed carpentry as a hobby. He taught me to "measure twice, cut once" and "if it's worth doing, it's worth doing right." Those early experiences witnessing his integrity in all aspects of life, from his role as Inspector General on base to building a deck at home, have pushed me to think ahead and to always put my integrity above all other performance measures.

Another hobby I picked up from my father was photography. In high school, I started shooting with his old 35-mm single lens reflex Pentax and joined the school newspaper as a photographer. My life goal at that time was to become either a photojournalist or a paramedic, which was influenced by participating in the Explorer ride-along program of the Boy Scouts of America. I had no academic ambitions and, despite having always tested well as "gifted and talented," I did not consider myself "smart." It was not until I received a $200 incentive award from the Science and Engineering Alliance, a consortium of four historically black colleges and universities and the Lawrence Livermore National Lab, that I even considered science, despite attending an engineering magnet high school. With that push, I upgraded my paramedic ambition to medical school and enrolled at Southern University and A&M College as a pre-med/biology major. (The award was later increased to $400, but I often chuckle at the fact that the nation bought a new scientist for a mere $200. Today, I'm an advocate for incentivizing science for young people, and I still thoroughly enjoy photography).

Later, a gentle push from my chemistry professor, Dr. Mildred Smalley, led me to change my major to chemistry, and yet another from my scholarship director, Dr. Diola Bagayoko, propelled me forward to graduate school to pursue a PhD. And yet, even while working toward a doctorate I was still struggling with self-awareness. It was one fortuitous day in the lab that I ran across a passage of prose on the Internet from Marianne Williamson (Williamson, 1992):

> Our deepest fear is not that we are inadequate. Our
> deepest fear is that we are powerful beyond mea-

sure. It is our light, not our darkness, that most frightens us. We ask ourselves, who am I to be brilliant, gorgeous, talented and fabulous? Actually, who are you not to be? You are a child of God. Your playing small doesn't serve this world. There's nothing enlightened about shrinking so that other people won't feel insecure around you. We were born to make manifest the glory of God that is within us; it is not just in some of us—it's in everyone! And as we let our own light shine, we unconsciously give other people permission to do the same. As we are liberated from our own fear, our presence automatically liberates others!

When I read this passage, sitting in that basement lab of Choppin Hall at Louisiana State University, and long before a movie further popularized these words, there was something about it that instantly resounded within me. I was a graduate student then, and it seemed to so well articulate many of my inner thoughts and feelings I had about myself. Many years later and as a professional and leader today, it still speaks to me.

As you will find, I did not turn out like so many others in my old neighborhood. I was blessed with an extremely supportive family and attended college and graduate school on scholarships and fellowships. And yet, I have always struggled with my accomplishments, especially in the face of the myriad disparities and discouragements that prevail in so many of our communities. Somehow, I have felt a need to compensate in some strange way, to minimize the good in my own life. For example, I can recall many times in the past when I was introduced to someone in a social setting as a chemistry professor. The response to this is usually something about how hard chemistry was for them in high school or maybe that they failed chemistry in college. I responded with some bumbling version of: "Oh, chemistry's no harder than anything else. Uh, I would suck at accounting. Heck, I can't even balance my checkbook."

Why would I make such a marginalizing (and untrue) comment about myself? Chemistry is challenging. Graduate school was hard, very hard, and it required every bit of dedication and perseverance that I could muster. This was the glory of God that was within me. But, how could I acknowledge, accept and be comfortable with this? Williamson's passage told me that there was a better response, and one that would at the same time liberate others. It is in that liberation of others that we find authentic leadership.

My postdoctoral and faculty appointments and recent leadership roles have led to an even greater sense of self-awareness. For example, a very junior staff member recently asked me to help her with her public speaking skills. Through the ensuing conversation, I realized her benchmark had been largely scripted by some of my public remarks at our student programming and public events. I quickly pointed out that we were in two different stages of our careers, that I should not be her current point of comparison, and I gave her some advice on improving in this area. And yet, I also realized that even when I was at her stage of career I was quite further along in the development of many skillsets.

That one conversation led to a prolonged time period of self-introspection, or what I think of as "gazing intently at one's own navel." In this, I questioned what experiences had helped me, and in turn, which of those experiences could also help others. In particular, I am certain that early participation in Toastmasters International (mandated by one of my college professors and mentors) helped me develop better public speaking skills than many of my peers. I had many other leadership and skill building opportunities and benefitted greatly from excellent mentors who invested heavily in me.

I've heard the term "mentor" defined as a wise or experienced person who helps a less experienced individual in something like an apprenticeship. However, a mentor is so much more than that. A great mentor has already learned not to play small and has discovered the light within themselves. They then invest in helping you make your own light shine in authentic ways.

And you should have many mentors, not just one. I have been blessed to have many truly great mentors, both women and men alike, and of any color, shape, creed, or size. From each of them I learn something different, and for that I am very thankful. One fantastic and wonderful authentic leader and mentor is Dr. Saundra McGuire. She is one of the brightest, most intelligent women I know. She is also one of the most graceful, warm-hearted, inspiring women I know. She is self-confident, self-assured, and assertive, while also being humble and transparent. There is a quality about her that truly does encourage me to be liberated from my fears. I also have several friends who are fantastic peer mentors. They encourage and motivate me, and they very often set me straight when I get out of line. From my mentors and along my journey, I've learned to be *me*, and to be authentically *me*. Now, I still code switch quite a bit, depending if I'm at home playing dominoes with my cousins or engaging leaders on campus on topics of inclusivity, but I've learned to be comfortable with me and to lead from a place of authenticity.

In all, my leadership style is deeply inspired by my life story and continuing to be shaped and reshaped by that life story. More recently, my story included a period of feeling devalued in my last academic appointment. Now, as a leader in a landscape where financial rewards are scarce and promotions are few and far in between, my past experience compels me to recognize the work of others with verbal praise and acknowledgement. I also try to reward others with small tokens of appreciation, including edible treats, and by pointing out specific accomplishments to others, including leadership on campus.

My authentic leadership style is also fueled by a desire to share the kinds of mentoring and coaching I have received along the way with others to help them succeed in their goals, particularly in higher education and in the science and engineering fields. I believe this is what led me to a career in education that began as a teacher. However, I don't think my current role as an administrator is much different. And I know that my authentic leadership will be in using my skills and gifts in a way that gives honor to my unique life story and enables others to do the same.

# References

Gardner, W. L., Cogliser, C. C., Davis, K. M., & Dickens, M. P. (2011). Authentic leadership: A review of the literature and research agenda. *The Leadership Quarterly, 22*(6), 1120-1145.

George, B., Sims, P., McLean, A. N., & Mayer, D. (2007). Discovering your authentic leadership. *Harvard Business Re-*

*view,* *85*(2), 129.

Shamir, B., & Eilam, G. (2005). "What's your story?" A life-stories approach to authentic leadership development. *The Leadership Quarterly, 16*(3), 395-417.

Williamson, M. (1992). *A return to love*: New York: HarperCollins.

# Leading From Within

Linda Johnson, PhD

Functioning in the capacity of a traditionally appointed or informally recognized leader, I have confidence that my foresight, personal and professional experiences, cognitive and practical skillsets, and professional credentials obtained through many personal and professional development programs will continue to guide me as I strive to be an effective leader. While the lessons learned, toolkits developed, and certifications attained are invaluable and instrumental in the adaptation and implementation of the various leadership theories, philosophies, approaches, and methodologies, this story—my story—will not focus on how I lead but, rather, how and when the foundation from which all of my conviction to lead was established. It was a time when I learned who I was, a time when I discovered my own internal, self-reaffirming, inextinguishable power source. It is the power source that gives me the courage to answer the call to lead.

To contextualize my state of mind at that time, I would like to use a concept that resonates with my sense of being, Janet Hagberg's model of personal power (Hagberg, 2002). This model defines personal power as our perceived ability to act and produce a specific external effect, thus effectively linking internal power to external power, power that influences others. As the internal and external powers developmentally and progressively link, personal power elevates. The levels of personal power reflect various levels of one's knowledge, confidence, experiences, and associations. The way in which these attributes temporally integrate define five stages of personal power: stage 1 – powerlessness; stage 2 – power by association; stage 3 – power by achievement; stage 4 – power by reflection; and stage 5 – power by purpose.

They say great leaders progress through the various stages as they are faced with life's challenges and their own ambition. Under normal conditions, one would presumably start at stage 1: powerlessness. Powerlessness is described as a stage of uncertainty, low self-esteem, lacking information, and the one that screamed my name, helpless but not hopeless. To move from stage 1 to stage 2 (power by association), one need to build self-esteem, confront their fears, develop their skillsets, *get* support, and *find allies*. While I was on track for developing my self-esteem and confronting my fears, I learned early that developing my skillsets was intertwined with getting support and finding allies. As a little black girl, for a time, my sense of hope simply transformed into a sense of helplessness. As a little black girl, getting support and finding allies forced me to rely on the other ways to move from stage 1: *appreciate myself* and *take responsibility*. At age 15, I did just that in spite of what appeared to me to be a culture designed to deprive, devalue, and disregard my very being and those like me.

At stage 1, one is expected to be timid, unsure, unaware of self, inexperienced, and maybe the low person on the totem pole. For me, those who knew they had my future in their hands viewed me differently. They viewed timid as incoherent, unsure as uneducated, inexperience as laziness and a lack of ambition, and the low person on the totem pole as the place where a black girl should be, a place where she ought to stay. So, during my stage 1, being timid, shy, and inexperienced was met with unfair judgement, exclusion, misinformation, and worst of all, a forced feeling of worthlessness. My story is her story. I had to work harder during that stage just to gain value, acknowledgment, and acceptance. I had to fight just to first look human and gain all of the rights and privileges pertaining to that. But even after gaining that, I still did not gain permission—permission to be who I was meant to be. A call from within empowered me to give myself permission. Sometimes the simplest decisions can trigger a cascade of events so mind-boggling, it can only be a gift from God.

Below is an excerpt from my journey towards attaining my personal power. This particular sequence of events was a turning point in my life. Internally, I moved from stage 1: powerlessness straight to stage 5: power by purpose. Becoming a leader was never my aspiration. Instead, enduring the many challenges of trying to be normal forced me to develop the characteristics of a leader. This was one of my first life-changing decisions weighted by the realization that being a little black girl was a disadvantage in life.

> Like many little black girls, I bused to (across at least six other school districts) and was passed through primary and secondary school; making little waves with just a hope to finish. While many of my teachers were black, most of the administrators or school counselors were white. As far as I can remember, there was no motivation to become anything more than what they thought I had come from—two parents educated up to the 9th grade. Without fully understanding when and why, I had been placed on a business track as I transitioned to junior high school.
>
> Not aware of anything else, I stayed in my appointed academic lane until one day the smell of sulfur in the school corridor piqued my curiosity. While everyone complained about the rotten egg smell, I sought out its origin and was amazed that it was an intentional

chemistry class product of a student activity. *Sign me up!* ran through my head. Later on that day, these same students appeared to be blissfully engaged in a biology class activity that was filled with chatter and clanking noises made by dissecting tools. My eyes widened as I peeked my head inside the classroom door. Again, in my head, I screamed, *Frogs! They're going to dissect frogs! Sign me up!* It turned out the scream was not in my head. However, not a bit aware of the disruption I caused, I fired off what seemed like a million and one questions. All leading to the question, "How do I sign up for this?" The biology teacher was excited about my excitement and said "No problem. Just sign up for the CP track in the counselor's office." CP? What is CP? Okay. While I was not sure about CP (college preparatory), I was certain about my desire to create strange chemical concoctions and to investigate the mysteries life, even though the frog was dead. As instructed, I innocently went to the school counselor.

About to burst with excitement, I told the counselor that I wanted to change from business to CP. With a dismissing glare, he looked in my eyes and said "You can't do that; we have you down as becoming a secretary." A little disappointed but still hopeful, I accepted that status and explained that I no longer wanted to be a secretary (I never did) and wish to be put on the CP track. "You can't," he said. "That track is for those who want to go to college." Okay, I will go to college then. Laughing, he told me that probably would never happen and that I should just focus on the secretarial schools. Feeling totally deflated, I left the office. But the next day, I saw the frogs again and the biology teacher let me stay awhile. The need to be one of those students was so overwhelming it forced me to talk to the counselor and try again to change my track. This time, he just flat out told me no and to drop it. "You can't change your track. Stop trying to be something you are not," he said. Why wouldn't he want me to be more than what I was? I felt worthless. Days went by, but I could not shake what I wanted and I was running out of time. The school year was ending, so the window to choose your track was closing fast. One day, the office secretary smiled at me as I was passing by. While the counselor had told me no, her smile gave me the courage to ask, "Why are some students on business track and others on CP? "Because that is what they chose," she said. *What they chose? I don't remember choosing*, I said in my head. "Can they change it?" I asked. "Yes, they can." "Does the counselor have to approve?" "Yes." "What if he doesn't want to?" I felt God had smiled down on me. She replied: "If your mother signs it, he has to send it through."

At that moment, my leadership skills began to develop, out of necessity. That quickly, I began to move out of stage 1. I strapped on an air of confidence. I became knowledgeable about what I needed to do. I associated myself with those of influence and completed all of the paperwork. Finally, I took the risk and signed my mother's name. You don't know my mother; that *was* a risk. I walked out of that room feeling an enormous sense of accomplishment. I went home a different person.

That simple act, was not only liberating but it gave me the confidence and strength to fight for myself. That decision not only created my own opportunities to be exposed to chemistry, biology, math, literature, art, and languages, it connected me to my power within. While I still face challenges, isolation, indifference, implicit and explicit biases, that experience taught me how to draw from who I am, not from how I'm treated. It is that inextinguishable internal force that leads me and allows me to lead others.

# Reference

Hagberg, J. O. (2002). *Real power: Stages of personal power in organizations* (3rd ed.). Salem, WI: Sheffield Publishing Company.

# Leadership Development for Women at HBCUs

Yolander Youngblood, PhD

The following represents a synopsis of my development as an authentic leader based upon a set of questions that every leader should ask herself (George et al., 2007).

## How I See Myself

I am Yolander "Renea" Youngblood, PhD. I have always thought of myself as a leader. For as long as I can remember I have been told that, as the eldest child, I had to lead by example. I was responsible for my younger siblings when my parents were away. If anything happened to both of my parents it would be my responsibility to determine what happened with my siblings. I have much respect for my parents and all leaders in general. I respect the leadership role; therefore, even if I do not like a person or their policies, I respect the leadership and follow the set rules and regulations.

I consider myself a transformational leader that communicates often with followers to ensure that desired goals and outcomes are conveyed effectively. I determine what motivates employees to enhance productivity. I focus on the big picture and delegate smaller tasks. This is what transformational leaders do. The effect is a lasting impact (Johnson, 2008). I believe this style of leadership is more fit for a modern or progressive organization (Eagly & Carli, 2007).

As scientists we are taught to learn from both the negative and positive results we gather from any study. In society, the best leaders learn from both successful and unsuccessful ventures (Shoemaker et al., 2013). One can then make the conclusion that scientists indeed can be great leaders.

Being a leader has a deeper purpose because this is one way of ensuring that things happen. For example, when something needs to be done, leaders take the initiative and make it happen. I use my leadership skills to serve my family. This is the legacy that I am leaving for my children. For example, my daughter wanted to be more social and develop more female friends. These friends are important because in the future she may seek advice from them before she comes to me. In order to put my mind at ease and feel more comfortable I needed to get to know these girls and their parents. In order to do this I created a group that served not only my and my daughter's interests but also those of the other girls and their parents. I created the "Princess Club." The Princess Club met regularly at church and sponsored events such as "Date with Daddy", "Etiquette Brunch," and informal but structured sessions about boys and dating. I got to know my daughter's future friends and their parents. This was important because everyone needs friends. Friends share common goals and experiences and influence each other. In order to help my daughter developed some lasting friendships I needed to provide some experiences that enabled her to do that.

I have a responsibility to leave a lasting positive legacy that provides support to my family, friends, and institution even after I am gone. This was exemplified when I gave my sister the opportunity to co-author an abstract with me. The opportunity greatly helped her career and allowed her to get a promotion at her school. I also served as "Big Sister" to my young cousin when she was a freshman in college. These activities ensure that if something happens to me, my children know that they are not alone and family members like these are there to help them. Family members often help just because you are family, but whenever one family member has invested a significant amount of time there is an even greater reward for that person or their offspring later down the road.

As the leader of an organization it is my responsibility to leave an organizational structure in place that will transition to the new leader and last until a new or different structure has been set.

## Core Values

The core values that have shaped who I am as a leader are God, family, respect, progressive thinking, and intelligence. God and family come first. I integrate everything else in my life around that, and then make time for church, staying scholarly active, respecting others, and surrounding myself with like-minded people.

## Events That Shaped My Leadership Personality

Events that shaped me include being the first of many things. I was the first black female valedictorian at my high school; and the first in my family to go away to college, move away, and get an apartment after college. Each of these steps was a milestone for me. I was quite proud of myself because I did these things without a role model or peer mentor. I learned independence. I learned that my success didn't depend on how much help I got from family or anyone else. My success depended on me. In actuality, I became a role model for the community. I showed them that a "good girl" from our community could do all of these things and still be a "good girl." My girlfriend gave me the pet name "Renegade" because I rejected convention. I always found her pet name odd because I see myself as outgoing, but careful. Yet others saw me as a renegade.

My experiences with mentors and major professors also helped shape my leadership personality. My male mentors and major professors were more directive in their leadership approach. This approach focused on the task or outcome desired and not the relationship between the mentor and mentee. A relationship might have developed as a side effect or byproduct. On the other hand, my female mentors and major professors had a leadership style that involved more coaching. Goals and expectations were communicated often. Fewer assumptions were made. This approach focused on the relationship and thus gave me the support I needed to complete the task as well as grow. These terms and definitions are based on those provided by the resource guide, "Practical Guide to Management for Postdocs and New Faculty" (2006). It is the latter approach that I use with my own student researchers.

As charter faculty for the Biotechnology Department and director of the Capital Area Biotechnology Partnership (CABP) at Harrisburg University, I was transformative when I used what I did know to figure out the many administrative details that I didn't know. I had the chance to move through some unfamiliar and unfriendly territory and build a program. As an administrator at a new institution, I found that there were many unknowns and little institutional structure. I endured much in the way of on-the-job training. I impressed myself in that I did more with less and was ever so creative in getting the job done. As charter faculty, my charge was to lead the effort and build a biotechnology program. I was not exactly given a budget. We had no equipment and no students yet. I needed to buy equipment for laboratories and add resources to help future students overcome barriers to enrolling in school, staying in school, and graduating on time. First I consulted with the Vice President for Academic and Student Affairs, university colleagues, external colleagues, biotech professionals, and community leaders, to determine what their goals were and then later to show that there were some common goal areas.

I searched for grant programs and submitted a proposal to the Pennsylvania Department of Community and Economic Development's 2+2+2 grant program. The university was touted as a community and economic venture; therefore, I believed that this funding source was appropriate. Scientists typically do not see sources such as this. I used the grant award I received to create a partnership. In order for any institution to have more stability and be more productive, that institution should have partnerships. The partnership I created was called the CABP. I was Director of the CABP. It was a partnership between Harrisburg University, Harrisburg Area Community College, Harrisburg Science and Technology High School, and industry partners that included Hershey Foods and the Pennsylvania Department of Agriculture. This partnership was unique for the area. It was the first university partnership fully funded with external funds that included a scientist, equipment, and support funds to overcome "barriers to success." It has lasted long after the initial grant funds and my term as director were exhausted.

# Person With the Greatest Impact on Leadership

I would say that my mother has probably had the greatest impact on me and on my life. She has served many roles. My mother was a teacher and my father a pastor/farmer/Bellsouth telephone laborer. My mother had six kids, worked as a teacher's aide, then stayed at home with the kids for 10 years. She still managed to work for 20 years as a full-time certified teacher, then retired. I find this remarkable because I know it was a juggling act. She always said, "Put family first, then make time for all those things that you want to do. Be patient, but keep moving in the direction of your goals." Her goal was to become a certified teacher. It took a few years because life kept throwing curve balls, but she accomplished her goal. She became a certified teacher and worked long enough to retire with her benefits. After her third child was in college she finally had the time and support to return to college part-time. She graduated just after her third child graduated. My grandparents were even able to come to the ceremony and celebrate.

My mother and I differ in that she is an introvert whereas I am an extrovert. She has a gentle way about her that can calm any outspoken or aggressive nature with ease. She is my advocate. Without her support from the beginning, I am not sure that I would have ventured into any other leadership roles. In her role as first lady of the church where my father pastors, she is forward thinking. She uses scripture to give support for her thinking. She once gave a talk and said that a wife's role was wherever she was needed. She said sometimes it is beside her husband to aid him. Sometimes it is behind him to push. Sometimes it is ahead of him to pull him in the right direction. That resonated with me not only in terms of marriage, but in terms of life for a woman. My place as a woman was wherever "I" deemed it necessary.

# My Integrated Life

I am a little different at home because my role is different. However, overall I am the same person. I do not have to shift gears. For instance, at home, I cook and often engage in social activities with family and close friends. I do not socialize often at work. I am more effective when I am authentic. Being authentic means that I use the skills and talents I have honed for decades along with the learned skills and strategies acquired from structured formal courses. I do pay a price sometimes for my authenticity. Initially I may be mistaken for being "too nice" and thus "flaky." This is dispelled when I use my ability to make others comfortable while still completing the task with the desired goal.

At Prairie View I found a way to incorporate informal student learning and informal faculty socializing in a formal course event. Each semester my botany class hosts a "Botanical Social" whereby students bring edible roots, stems, leaves, and fruits. Faculty, who are often unable to get out for lunch, are invited to come and ask questions regarding the structure and make-up of these plant parts. Students are required to answer questions in a nonthreatening way. Students then take their scheduled test after the event (usually the next day). I get to interact with the faculty and they get to interact with me. Socials help generate a feeling of warmth. This is important when trying to get people to hear your message (Cuddy et al., 2013). We now all look forward to the event.

## How I Stay Grounded

I surround myself with close friends and family. My closest friends have been there for more than 15 years. They have seen me under several different circumstances. They know who I am. My friends keep me grounded in that they allow me to be myself.

My husband reminds me that I must have time to spend with my family. There is an appropriate amount of time to put into work and pursue additional opportunities. Sometime long hours may be necessary, but long hours should not happen at the expense of family. While I strive to do so much more because I am passionate, I must remember to be thankful for where I am and enjoy the moment. Also, it is okay to continue to make small extrinsic moves. In an effort to stay true to my authenticity, I keep my support team close. I continue to take my kids to games and I continue to lean on my husband at home.

## Importance of Understanding My Story

Intelligent followers don't just follow. They must understand their leader. They must have a sense of trust and understanding. They must feel a connection and a level of comfort with the leader, otherwise they will not follow (Cuddy et al., 2013.) This is true for both students and colleagues. I like to determine what motivates people and then use this knowledge to enhance productivity. I focus on the big picture, but delegate smaller tasks to others.

## Importance of Women Leaders

Many women in higher education leadership have been discriminated against. They have gained success in leadership roles in spite of many adversities. They have used these adversities and found hidden opportunities (Diehl, 2014). Women bring diversity. By diversity I mean a different perspective. During an interview with Frances Hesselbein, she spoke openly about the importance of women in leadership. Frances Hesselbein is a former CEO of Girl Scouts, Founding CEO of Peter Drucker's Leadership Institute, and author of several books. She is also a recipient of the 1998 Presidential Medal of Freedom. She believes that the differences in gender, race, culture, and life experiences bring a different perspective that should be acknowledged, not hidden away. This diversity strengthens the leadership team and the organization (Reiss, 2013). Businesses now realize that it is good to have diversity in leadership teams. A 2011 Lord Davies report showed that businesses with women in the leadership team have a four percent higher return on sales (Almond, 2013). As scientists we teach that diversity is important to the universe because it allows the species, the community, etc. to adapt to seen and unforeseen changes. In order to adapt it is best that there be some variability (Mader & Windelspecht, 2012). This is significant. So when it comes to leadership and diversity, scientists have a deep understanding of the significance.

Women are also important as leaders because they can change things for future women.

## Leadership Advice for Junior Faculty at an HBCU

1. The first opportunity you have to lead is in the classroom. Make it count. In order to make it count it is imperative to tie topics to current day issues (for the department, institution, or community), or real-world experience, etc.

2. The second opportunity to lead is within the department. Share

those ideas from external conferences with individual colleagues the day before a departmental meeting. Share over coffee or at the copier machine. Ideas may include a proposed event for the department to sponsor or a suggestion for an existing event. These occasions are when people are not guarded and usually they feel as if you value there opinion. Be aware of the vibes you receive from them and act accordingly.

3. The third opportunity is actually sharing that idea in a relevant way in a meeting, when things are recorded.

4. The fourth opportunity to lead is via committees. It is important to wait for the right opportunity to come to you. Some opportunities require so much energy, and/or effort and/or navigation of institutional politics that attempting to lead by committee may not be beneficial at the time. Timing is important. But, while you are waiting for an opportune time, prepare yourself. Keep up with everyday campus concerns and issues. Read the faculty senate reports. Learn the political landscape of your college. This is very important because of the "You must provide proper respect" culture of many HBCUs. Then when the time is right, you department chair or even the dean will ask for faculty input. When you provide that feedback, always follow the chain of command via a paper trail, and support your feedback with evidence.

5. Fifth, and lastly, you can gain favor and opportunities to lead from your chair and awareness from other campus leaders by attending workshops with your chair that no one else wants to attend.

Once you have consistently done these things, you will be asked to lead a committee or project that nobody else wants. This will be an important project, but no senior faculty member will want the hassle of leading it. An example is taking on the leadership of the department's research symposium. Accepting the offer to lead will be your time to shine.

# References

Almond, S. (2013). Gender diversity in leadership is key to business success. *The Guardian*. Retrieved from http://www. theguardian.com/sustainable-business/gender-diversity-leadership-business-success.

Cuddy, A.J.C., Kohut, M., & Neffinger, J. (2013). Connect, then lead. *Harvard Business Review, 91*(7/8), 55-61.

Eagly, A. H., & Carli, L. L. (2007). Through the Labyrinth: The truth about how women become leaders (pp.161-182). Boston: Harvard Business School Press.

George, B., Sims, P., McLean, A., & Mayer, D. (2007). Discovering your authentic leadership. *Harvard Business Review*, *85*(2).

Johnson, R. (2008). 5 Different Types of Leadership Styles. Retrieved from http://smallbusiness.chron.com/5-different-types-leadership-styles-17584.html.

Mader, S., & Windelspecht, M. (2015). *Biology* (12th ed.). New York: NY: McGraw-Hill Publishers.

Practical Guide to Management for Postdocs and New Faculty (2nd ed.). (2006). Retrieved from http://www.hhmi.org/

labmanagement.

Reiss, R. (2013). America's greatest leader shares her wisdom on leadership, women, millennials and civility. Retrieved from http://www.forbes.com/sites/robertreiss/2013/09/30/americas-greatest-leader-shares-her-wisdom-on-leadership-women-millennials-and-civility/.

Shoemaker, P.J.H., Krupp, S., & Howland, S. (2013). Strategic leadership the essential skill. *Harvard Business Review* (January–February Issue). http://hbr.org/2013/01/strategic-leadership-the-esssential-skills/ar/1.

# Part II

# Theory, Practice, and Experience

# The Seven Virtues of Leadership

Suzanne Seleem, PhD

I was never inspired to compete or apply for a leadership role at work or in any community or charity activities that I participated in because in my mind I equated leadership and leaders solely with politics and politicians. To me "leadership" involved many things that were just not in me . . . but I was wrong.

Through my informal interactions with my students and colleagues as an advisor, mentor, and/or a friend, I discovered the real hardcore characteristics of what I consider a successful and influential leader. Neglecting order of importance, they are:

**1. Sincerity.** A leader should be genuinely sincere about everyone and everything she/he is in charge of. One cannot fake it. Human beings and other creatures are born with this deep-rooted instinct for differentiating between sincere and insincere fellow creatures and they are usually right.

**2. Honesty and Integrity.** If one's honesty and integrity are not priorities to guard and protect, one should avoid any leadership role. Attacks, sometimes fatal, will pour down from everywhere, from friends and foes alike.

**3. Fairness.** One cannot assume the role of a leader without being fair to all. It is very difficult sometimes to stand by your opponents, but if they are right nothing else matters and all other differences should play no role.

**4. Selflessness.** If one seeks a leadership role for personal gain only, she/he should drop it; neither the position nor one's role will last.

**5. Decision-Maker and Action/Calculated Risk-Taker.** No leader can survive if she/he is not capable or cannot be responsible for making decisions and taking action when needed. A shrewd successful leader should realize that some risks are great hidden opportunities that are sometimes neglected out of fear of failure.

**6. Emotional Intelligence.** Emotional intelligence is a life-long training and sometimes a struggle for many. A leader should be mature enough to learn from her/his mistakes and failures in order to overcome them in the future. After all, failures can be the best lessons that we learn from.

**7. Empathy.** The first role of a leader is to be able to be empathetic toward others, and this goes beyond being sympathetic only. This is not an easy role and does not come naturally to many due to many circumstances that they have had to go through. But out of sincere care and compassion for others, empathy can quickly be embedded in one's character and soul.

After identifying these seven important characteristics of leadership through several intensive training opportunities but, most importantly, from the help of others who out of their kind hearts and souls shared their experiences with me and stood by me whenever I needed to find my way and put my career on the right path, I found out that I possess the bases of the above characteristics, and working to strengthen some of them and myself is a task that I look forward to achieve in my lifetime. Now I look forward to serve as a leader in every capacity and at any opportunity presented to me or even one that comes to my knowledge, where I know I can be of help and make a positive impact and difference.

Leadership to me, now, is a badge of honor for serving others to the best of my abilities. I am proud to honor and carry it.

# An Evolving Voice in Leadership

## Leyte L. Winfield, PhD

Assisting women of color to advance in various science fields is a social justice issue that resonates with many in our nation. For more than 12 years, I have contributed to this effort as a scholar, teacher, mentor, and now a leader. I have a rather unusual blend of leadership experience through my positions at Spelman College, a commission in the U.S. Army (resigned in 2009), and service to various community organizations (Changing a Generation Board of Trustees and Merit Badge Counselor for Boy Scouts of America). My leadership at Spelman has involved a mixture of college committees and various directorships. In my current role as chair of the Department of Chemistry and Biochemistry, I have gained presence, learned to collaborate, and pursued work/life balance. These attributes will be addressed herein, as they are essential to who I am becoming as a leader. But what is the archetype of an effective leader? Many have toyed with the idea without converging on a unified belief on leadership. Indeed, there are many voices in leadership and mine continues to evolve (George, 2007). With any of the models that have been established, one must embody the traits with genuine confidence in them (George, 2007). That is to say, one must be convinced of their worth as an individual and believe that they add value to the space they occupy. Genuine confidence in one's unique self is not to be confused with false confidence or that which wavers based on the situation. It is what informs the individual that they possess the skillset, or the capacity to gain the skillset, needed for the job despite failure and setback. One might say that this type of confidence in oneself brings forth authentic leadership. Therefore, an authentic leader is one who can exploit their experiences, passion, and commitment to a cause to accomplish a task (George, 2007). These individuals are able to balance intrinsic and extrinsic motivation while leveraging the support needed from others. Most importantly, authentic leaders understand their life's journey as an integral force that shapes their approach to a situation. I recall struggling with my given name, Leyte, as a youth and how the acceptance of the name has shaped who I am today.

The Province of Leyte (pronounced Lay-TE) in the Philippines is one of the most beautiful places in the world. I have met several individuals from that region of the globe who testify to its enchantment and splendor. The land is covered with lush tropical foliage and beautiful flowers (including orchids, my favorite). The island has beautiful beaches and an abundance of waterfalls. I was named after this very exotic place, but would not understand the significance of this until later in life.

As a kid, my name was the bane of my existence. I often pondered, "How could my mom give me this awful name?" No one could pronounce it based on the spelling. To make matters worse, my mom pronounces it Lay-Ta instead of Lay-TE. Eventually, I shied away from correcting the mispronunciation of my name, as it brought more ridicule than reverence. Kids would say "See ya lay-ta" or "You want some Now or Lay-tas?" relating my name to the popular saying and the candy of that time.

After a while, I began introducing myself by my middle name and began saving money to make the change official. I was no longer Leyte but now my middle name, Taja. Nevertheless, the Taja phase of my life was short-lived. As Taja, I was feisty and could roll my neck and eyes in unison while slinging some sarcastic comment your way. Taja was quick to speak and slow to think. Taja hung with the wrong people and did all the wrong things. Taja had dreams, but no plan, direction, or purpose. In short, Taja was not who I was to become. She was not Leyte.

Leyte also had dreams. But unlike Taja, Leyte was ambitious, driven, and convinced she would succeed. Leyte was shy, but assertive. She was a bit sassy, but loving, as well as goofy but astute. If you were to find yourself in Leyte's company, or if you were fortunate enough to be counted among her friends, you would be found in a blessed place. I am so happy to have evolved into all that my mom knew Leyte would become. I celebrate my mother for having the wisdom (even at 16 years old) to give me a name that resonates with my true self. The name fills me with pride and I think of my mom lovingly each time I say to someone, "It's pronounced Lay-TE and it represents a beautiful place."

Indeed, my acceptance of who I am and the keen awareness of my potential are the foundation of who I am becoming as a leader. In reframing this life experience and pursuing authentic leadership, I am evolving into the leader I'm purposed to be, the woman called to lead. Here I share key strategies that have been instrumental in my evolutions: managing my non-verbal expressions of power; learning to collaborate; and pursuing balance.

## Managing Nonverbal Expressions of Power

As an introvert, I must often remind myself to loosen up and not to appear withdrawn in professional situations. "Open up your body, smile, and do not cross your arms" were the mental reminders I would evoke early in my career. That is, instead of thinking small and holding my body in a closed posture, I learned to *think big*. Being mindful of my demeanor has been instrumental in my ability to gain influence and successfully implement proposed initiatives. These nonverbals have been correlated to one's perception of power and ability to engage with others (Cuddy, 2012). In the TEDx Talk entitled "Your Body Language Shapes Who You Are," Amy Cuddy indicates that often we are judged not by what we say, but by how we say it or how we present the conversation. The latter she calls *presence*, which is related to the level of passion, confidence, and enthusiasm displayed in a given situation. Presence is also indicative of one's ability to captivate their audience while demonstrating a level of authenticity and comfort with the situation. In short, presence impacts how an individual is received. As a leader, this trait in particular will impact your ability to influence those you lead and to effectively convey the information. That is, having presence is a key ingredient to being perceived as having authority.

There is a Christian proverb which states, "A joyful heart brightens one's face, but a troubled heart breaks the spirit" (Proverbs 15:13, Common English Bible). Cuddy, like the Bible, suggests that our minds change our bodies. She goes on to suggest that power posing can modulate key hormones, upregulate testosterone, and downregulate cortisol, which leads to increased feelings of power. She suggests practicing the poses prior to entering a situation that could be threatening or one in which a high-low power differential exists between parties involved in the exchange, such as situations in which one might engage a supervisor. The fundamental concept of the power pose involves expanding the space and area your body occupies. Cuddy et al. indicate that in high-stakes social evaluation, characterized by a significant power difference between the individuals involved, the individuals often complement the demeanor of the other (Cuddy, Wilmuth, & Carney, 2012). That is, if one party assumes a high power pose, the other party will assume a low power pose. A more relaxed body posture during such exchanges places an individual at ease and produces a less timid disposition. It is important that leaders are able to master these nonverbals to set the tone for engagement. Doing so has been an instrumental part of my leadership journey.

I have become better able to present myself with authenticity, confidence, and passion. Although my introverted nature is ever with me, practicing appropriate nonverbal behaviors allows me to present myself as one having the skillset needed for success and secure in the power that has been entrusted to me. Beginning with accepting my given name, as discussed in the opening, I have learned how to present myself as a winner. My advice to women who have been called to lead is that how you say it is as important as what you are saying. To gain influence and to operate effectively in a given role, how you present yourself goes a long way toward ensuring that you are well received as a leader.

## Learning to Collaborate

"If you want to go fast, go alone. If you want to go far, go together (African Proverb)." This saying holds a powerful lesson on collaboration that is beneficial to successful leadership. Collaboration not only provides the manpower needed for a given initiative, but it also empowers the team by allowing members to take ownership in what is to be accomplished. To empower a team member is to allow the individual to demonstrate authority in completing a given assignment. It can lead to reduced work related stress and positive job performance outcomes (Newman, 2015; de Klerk, 2014). Empowerment works in concert with presence to produce effective leadership. Where presence allows the leader to present themselves with authority and confidence, through empowerment the leader is able to demonstrate confidence in those being led. In my role as department chair, collaboration was essential to the initiatives being proposed. What was unexpected was the level of collaboration that was requested by faculty for day-to-day decisions. Nevertheless, the collaborative approach to all aspects has resulted in faculty support for department initiatives, increased faculty participation, and effective delegation of tasks. A drawback of this method is that it may take time to gain consensus before a decision is made. Despite the time required, collaboration is needed to ensure a productive and supported process.

I recall making an autocratic decision. Although I felt that most faculty members would support the decision, I later discovered that this was not the case. The process had to come to a halt so that the situation could be discussed. Everyone ultimately supported the initial decision, but first needed the opportunity to provide input on the situation. While this caused "my" timeline to be altered, I think the break allowed us to ensure that all needed voices were represented. This was important, as not having consensus on this particular project could have invalidated the final results. In this case, my ability to exercise "individualized consideration" helped to ensure that everyone was on the same page and that our work would not be in vain (Eagly & Carli, 2007). In the end, I learned that collaboration does not mean losing as an individual, but winning as a team.

My advice to women called to lead would be to pursue every opportunity to involve team members fully in the process from planning to implementation. Assure your team that their contributions are valued by empowering them to lead in their own way. The outcome of collaboration will be more fulfilling than going it alone.

## Pursuing Balance

> Equilibrium is defined as a state in which opposing forces or influences are balanced. Although the academic scientific enterprise prides itself on understanding these forces in laboratory systems, it has fallen short in recognizing and remedying the imbalance between the demands of career and those of personal life. This imbalance contributes to extreme professional sacrifices and lowered retention of many talented individuals striving for successful careers in science. (Richmond and Rohlfing, 2013)

Work-life imbalance has been attributed to increased healthcare costs, delayed parenting, work-related conflict, and career burnout (Amstad, 2015). It is not selfish to pursue work-life balance. Self-care is important to being effective as a leader. The things that make you human should not be sacrificed in the name of being a scholar. Eagly and Carli discussed the changing trends in work hours, particular the ratio that exists between those of men and of women (2007). At my first COACh (Committee on the Advancement of Women Chemists) workshop (an organization originally developed to promote leadership among women chemists), the disparity and misperception was described in an interesting yet troubling way. The facilitator indicated that a woman who arrives at work early and leaves late is viewed as performing adequately. If, however, that same woman adjusts her work hours to an acceptable eight hours, she is viewed as slacking. This is the case even when her work productivity does not change. This seems to suggest that women are still required to outperform their male counterparts in order to be considered, not as equal to them, but as acceptable. Adding to this, it has been shown that women experience lower levels of job satisfaction due to impaired work-life balance.

Knowing this, I decided to pursue success on my own terms. I celebrate the highs and press through the lows. I recognize the "value-added" contributions I make to my institution and actively engage in bringing visibility to my successes (publishing, blogging, utilizing social media and presentations, mentoring, etc.). For me, however, pursuing excellence on my own terms did not coincide with a healthy work-life balance. As a young professor, I was very proud of the amount of time I put into my career. My day would begin at 5:30 so that I could make it to the office by 7 a.m. I would leave around 5:30 p.m., pick up my son from aftercare, and go home to continue to work until midnight. After receiving tenure, I felt this inexplicable lull. While others were rejoicing, I was wondering what it all meant. After many years of this imbalance, I realized that my energy state was impaired. Therefore, these are the steps I'm taking to reclaim balance.

My son is on my calendar. His activities take priority, no exceptions and no cancelations.

I delegate as much as I can.

I try not to bring work home; sometimes this means working late.

I go to church.

I take a dance class; hobbies are important.

I leave the office for lunch.

To maintain productivity, I create a daily calendar which I strictly follow. If I allot 30 minutes to respond to emails, those messages not responded to in that time are tabled until the next scheduled email time. To maintain a connection to faculty, I work in 45-minute blocks with frequent 15-minute breaks. This also acts as a buffer for unexpected events that require my immediate attention. When working on a project that requires concentrated time, a full day may be devoted to that activity, with the 15-minute breaks being incorporated after 60 minutes. It has proven useful to me to inform others of my availability using an automated email reply or voicemail, especially when I will not be available to respond to messages during extended period of times, even when I am in the office. In addition to my scheduling my day, my son has been instrumental in helping me achieve balance. He keeps me accountable to my new life goals by gently (and not so gently at times) reminding me when I've been locked in my home office for too long. We both are mindful to have breakfast together on Saturday mornings and a sit-down dinner every Sunday. Nevertheless, work-life balance for me is a work in progress. Faith is important, family is important, and I am important. It must all be nurtured for me perform at my best. My advice to women called to lead is that work-life balance is necessary to be an effective leader.

Knowing my authentic self has taught me to embrace and celebrate all that I am: a woman; a mother; and scientist. All three intertwine to fuel my passion as a leader ensuring that women of African descent not only have a place, but also have an opportunity to excel in STEM (science, technology, engineering, and mathematics) fields. Through my various leadership experiences, I have gained clarity on the responsibility of power and how power can be leveraged to ensure both my success and the success of those I lead. Through this self-awareness, however, I understand that I am still a work in progress and my leadership voice is still evolving.

# References

Amstad, F. T., Meier, L. L., Fasel, U., Elfering, A., & Semmer, N. K. (2011). A meta-analysis of work–family conflict and various outcomes with a special emphasis on cross-domain versus matching-domain relations. *Journal of Occupational Health Psychology, 16*(2), 151.

Barsh, J., & Cranston, S. (2011). *How remarkable women lead: The breakthrough model for work and life.* Crown Business: New York.

COACh, Committee on the Advancement of Women Chemists. (n.d.). Retrieved April 16, 2014, from http://coach.uoregon.edu/coach/index.php?id=47.

Csikszentmihályi, M. (1998). *Finding flow: The psychology of engagement with everyday life.* New York: Basic Books.

Cuddy, A. J. (2012). Your body language shapes who you are. Retrieved November 22, 2015, from https://www.ted.com/speakers/amy_cuddy.

Cuddy, A. J., Wilmuth, C. A., & Carney, D. R. (2012). The benefit of power posing before a high-stakes social evaluation. Retrieved April 28, 2014, from Harvard Business School Working Paper, No. 13-027: http://nrs.harvard.edu/urn-3:HUL.InstRepos:9547823.

de Klerk, S., & Stander, M. W. (2014). Leadership empowerment behaviour, work engagement and turnover intention: The role of psychological empowerment. *Journal of Positive Management*, 5(3), 28-45.

George, B., Sims, P., McLean, A. N., & Mayer, D. (2007). Discovering your authentic leadership. *Harvard Business Review*, February:1-8.

Newman, A., Schwarz, G., Cooper, B., & Sendjaya, S. (2015). How servant leadership influences organizational citizenship behavior: The roles of LMX, empowerment, and proactive personality. *Journal of Business Ethics*, 1-14.

Richmond, G. L., & Rohlfing, C. M. (2013). Work-life balance. *Personnel Review,* 41(6), 813-831.

# Succession Planning In Higher Education

Christa Ellen Washington, PhD

## Leadership, Diversity and Succession Planning in Higher Education

At present, women and racial minorities have considerable trouble moving into leadership roles in higher education. Literature related to succession planning in higher education is significantly limited. According to a 2007 report by the American Council on Education (ACE), the numbers of women and minorities in presidential positions at colleges and universities have not increased significantly since 1998. Not only has there been little movement in terms of the presidency, but these groups are also underrepresented in other senior administrative positions such as deans, provosts, and vice presidents. Due to the low numbers of women and minorities assuming leadership roles, the need to develop "succession planning models" should be considered to help increase the number of minorities in leadership. Projections of leadership turnover indicate as much as 50 percent among higher administrators within higher education beginning in 2014 (Klein & Salk, 2013). Succession planning can help institutions recognize current employees who have not only talent, but the potential to move into leadership roles. The ACE report highlights the fact that almost half of all college presidents are age 61 or older, which offers opportunities for renewal.

As a result of these data, ACE and others recommend that more women and minorities be considered for presidencies, and more women and minorities should be promoted to chief academic officer positions, the traditional preparation for the presidency. In order to address these deficiencies, institutions of higher education should consider the following factors for developing a succession plan: (1) selecting an interim replacement; (2) identifying the skills and characteristics of potential candidates; (3) recognizing possible internal candidates; and (4) selecting leadership development models. At the present time, the Chronicle for Higher Education shows that there are currently eight sitting college/university presidents who have tenures of 30 years or more in that role. This paper will introduce the idea of succession planning and suggest strategies for implementing succession plans.

## Defining and Understanding Succession Planning

Succession planning is a systematic process for leadership preparation for the future. This process is a way to create a diverse pool of leaders who are well-prepared to fill leadership positions at an institution. Henri Fayol (1841-1925) was one of the first to write about succession planning. Fayol (as cited in Rothwell, 2010) argued that organizations and institutions are responsible for developing leaders. Charan, Drotter, and Noel (2001) defined succession planning as "perpetuating the enterprise by filling the pipeline with high-performing people to assure that every leadership level has an abundance of these performers to draw from, both now and in the future" (p. 167). The goal of succession planning in higher education is to prepare individuals to assume key leadership roles when people retire, transfer, or find new opportunities outside of an institution of higher education. The Society of Human Resource Management refers to succession planning as preparation, not selection. Despite succession planning models' success in the private sector, these approaches have yet to take root in higher education (Stripling, 2011). Eventually there will be leadership vacancies to fill at all institutions of higher learning. How will higher education groom future leaders? Will succession planning change the face of leadership in higher education?

## Succession Planning in Universities and Colleges

Due to tradition and culture, succession planning in higher education is not a formalized process. The trend has been that colleges and universities assume that their next leader (i.e., president) will come from outside the institution. This rationale is sometimes supported by the institutions' desire to go in a different direction, thereby forgoing logical successors on campus—e.g., the provost, vice presidents, and deans. There are also other explanations as to why higher education has not developed succession planning models. One reason for the lack of consideration for succession planning is that, in academia, there is little internal operational focus on leadership (Davis, 2008). Another reason is the belief that only a national search can address affirmative action concerns regarding the selection process. A third reason is that institutions tend to rely on national searchers to identify potential leadership candidates (Lapovsky, 2006). A leader-in-waiting at most universities or colleges may be viewed with suspicion and antagonism by faculty, staff, and students. In most cases, higher education institutions look externally to fill the president's position. However, since there is a projected leadership crisis in higher education, institutions must begin to address the need to develop a pipeline for leadership roles. To prevent a dearth of viable internal candidates each time a vacancy occurs, Stripling (2011) believes that boards of trustees should encourage presidents and chief academic officers to identify and groom potential successors for their roles. Succession planning in higher education should be inclusive and intentional. If institutions of higher education hope to find success in developing a plan, they must be clear about whom they will prepare for leadership roles and what type of training and development these individuals will receive, as well as identifying what resources are needed to be successful in the overall process. More importantly, if institutions fail to develop succession plans, the demands of identifying new leadership will become more difficult. Current leaders in higher education are beginning to leave at high rates and it is imperative for institutions to be prepared for the exit of top leadership (Parkman & Beard, 2008).

Despite the growing need for and interest in succession planning, many institutions are still ill-prepared to handle changes in leadership that may be short-term or long-term placements. To begin the process of developing succession planning models, higher education should consider replacement planning as well as talent management. Although replacement planning focuses on emergency backups to fill critical leadership positions, this process of thinking can help to develop more long-term plans for succession of leadership. Additional benefits of considering talent management include focusing on attracting the best talent (most productive), developing the best talent (promotable people), and retaining the best talent (putting the right people in the right positions) (Rothwell, 2008).

The following questions are concluding thoughts for institutions to consider:

-If the institution lost one of the key leaders suddenly, how quickly could a replacement be found?

-What is the institution's plan for leaders planning to retire?

-How many current employees could serve as replacements or backups, and how long would it take to prepare them for the job?

If the answers to these questions reveal uncertainty or an inability to deal with sudden or planned changes in leadership, then this is an issue that should generate interest as well as planning regarding the future and preparation for new leadership. Developing a pipeline for leadership is of no value if the plan is not implemented and does not include action to improve the readiness of individuals to be trained to assume leadership roles. It is important that the top talent is encouraged to pursue opportunities that will continue to build on their competencies to prepare for promotion (Rothwell, 2011).

## What Are the Next Steps?

Institutions of higher education can consider the proposed toolkit as a viable source for developing a succession plan. This plan integrates common succession planning methods with other targeted efforts that provide continuous career development. The following three steps are based on the current literature and can help build and possibly strengthen succession planning models in higher education:

**Step One:** Develop top talent with skills, attributes, and experiences that will align well with administrative positions (i.e., dean, provost, or president). Current administrators should meet to discuss the process for selecting individuals to participate in leadership development. The group should identify questions that assess an individual's attributes, capabilities, needs, desires, and potential for becoming a leader.

**Step Two:** Identify short-term and long-term needs to help develop and implement the best plan of action. Based on the needs of the institution, the model should provide job-specific training for levels of leadership.

**Step Three**: Develop a multilevel succession planning model. Recognizing that leadership roles vary in higher education, it is important to develop a tiered approach for how the training and planning will be implemented. This toolkit proposes three levels of succession planning:

a. Lower-Level Management—Focus on improving fundamental leadership skills and exposure to different tasks and duties (Examples: associate professors, assistant and associate directors)

b. Mid-Level Management—Identify a cohort of high-performing individuals and assign cross-functional work and larger projects, and provide them with greater exposure to institutional processes (i.e., strategic planning, institutional budgeting, etc.). (Examples: directors, department chairs, etc.)

c. High-Level Management—Have top-performing individuals work closely with administrators in the capacity of an administrative fellow and provide input for key decisions.

(Examples: dean, vice provosts, etc.)

Succession planning is more than identifying individuals for leadership positions. When considering new leaders, it is important to identify individuals who will offer new perspectives and new ideas. This toolkit focuses on providing a general guide for developing and retaining top-performing individuals at colleges and universities through mentoring, special projects, and specific leadership training. Garmen and Glawe's (2004) research suggests that succession planning helps to improve job satisfaction, higher individual and departmental performance, and increased retention of high-performing employees. Overall, this toolkit has the potential to offer long-term benefits for succession planning in higher education by providing training and opportunities to guide the development of future leaders of higher education.

Women can become candidates or gain the attention of key decision makers by first challenging themselves to gain exposure. It is important for women who desire to advance in higher education to identify effective mentors and sponsors. Also, there are programs that have been known to assist women in understanding the challenges and how to best navigate the barriers. Some of these programs are HERS, Bridges of UNC-North Carolina, and ACE Leadership, to name a few.

# References

American Council on Education. (2007). *The American College President*. Washington, DC: American Council on Education, Center for Policy Analysis.

Charan, R., Drotter, S., & Noel, J. (2011). *The leadership pipe-*

*line: How to build the leadership powered company.* San Francisco, CA: Jossey-Bass.

Chronicle for Higher Education. (2013). *The Chronicle Review.* Washington, DC.

Davis, E. B., Jr. (2008, July 18). Colleges need to offer clear paths to leadership. *The Chronicle of Higher Education.* Retrieved from http://chronicle.com/Colleges-Need-to-Offer-Clear/16225.

Garman, A. N., & Glawe (2004). Succession planning. *Consulting Psychology Journal: Practice and Research, 56*(2), 119-128.

Klein, M. F., & Salk, R. J. (2013). Presidential succession planning: A qualitative study in private higher education. *Journal of Leadership & Organizational Studies, 20*, 335-345.

Lapovsky, L. (2006, November 21). California's community colleges struggle to recruit and retain president. *The Chronicle of Higher Education.* Retrieved from http://chronicle.com/article/California-Community/7524.

Parkman, A., & Beard, R. (2008). Succession planning and the imposter phenomenon in higher education. *CUPA-HR Journal, 59*(2), 29036.

Rothwell, W. J. (2011). Replacement planning: a starting point for succession planning and talent management. *International Journal of Training and Development, 15*(1), 87-99.

Rothwell, W. J. (2010). *Effective succession planning.* New York, NY: AMACOM.

Rothwell, W. J. (2008). Next generation talent management. *HRM Review, 8*(10), 10-16.

Stripling, J. (2011, September 25). The graying presidency: Major universities face imminent problems of succession planning. *The Chronicle of Higher Education.*

# Leading Across the Academic Warzone: Emerging Stronger Than You Could Have Ever Imagined

Bianca Garner, PhD

"Just say yes, and this will all go away."

In the midst of highly charged meetings, with everyone trying to get their point across, I could hear the words so clearly. There was such anger and determination in the person's eye. I just stopped and really looked and knew. This was my defining moment in leadership. I had done nothing wrong but was being asked to act as if I had. I knew the decisions I made and the way I carried myself would live on long after the meeting was closed.

An academic setting is a unique environment. Like the United States, departments and programs have boundaries. In most cases, the boundaries are clearly defined with markers so that everyone understands what belongs to whom. Crossing boundaries is usually met with skepticism, opposition and, sometimes, outright hostility. In academic institutions, space and the allocation of space is a landmine. No one ever has enough and there is never enough for everyone. Reallocating space can cause a war that can disrupt working conditions and can never be healed. In this instance, the department had received funding and was mandated to create a research laboratory from existing space. The decision was made to remove space from one program and to allocate it to my department. Thus began a war that I had not asked for, but was still called to lead through. This is when leadership is hardest, but it is true definition of leadership.

A lot of people want to lead. They at some point in time think that they can do the job better than the current leader. In their minds, they see so many wrongs and have the exact answer needed to fix them. With rose-colored glasses, they see only a few of the demands and issues of leadership, but know that they can fix them. In this vision, everyone is working on the same page. You are the choirmaster and everyone is singing on key.

Not everyone, however, will sing on key. Some will be disruptive and create an environment where discourse is key. This is the war zone and reality of leadership. People will not agree with your decisions. People will not support your decisions. And, sometimes, people will work against those decisions. In the academy, decisions can be made for you and leaders must carry them out to the best of their abilities.

In that moment, I could have acquiesced, even though I had not done anything wrong. Leading became tough. I had to make a decision that would change how I was viewed and change my ability to lead. In the face of such animosity, it is easy for a leader to waiver. However, to make an issue go away and to just fix it comes at a great cost. Also, it is easy to stoop to someone else's level, making the issue personal. A true leader, though, can never do that. A leader can never let an issue become about his or her feelings, especially when that leader is a woman. Even though the leader has every right to want to make it personal or react instantly, doing either means that power and influence are diminished. This results in one's becoming an emotional wreck, and others will view this as an inability to lead. The bottom line is that it does not matter how the situation came to be; what matters is how one responds.

So, I looked over at the individual who was challenging me. In my mind, I knew if I just said to the whole room of people, my peers within the division, that I would refuse what the college had said and not take the space, it would all be over. The individual and I could go back to being friends within our boundaries. On the other hand, I could face war, as was implied. I knew that for the sake of my departmental faculty and my career, I could not waiver. The individual knew I did not like such hostility and was counting on me to back down. However, a leader understands what is at stake and makes the decision. Therefore, I said "no" and prepared for whatever ugliness followed.

And it was ugly, but an interesting thing happened. I had been so focused and busy fighting that I did not realize the support I had. A true leader can never win the battle alone. One must have faculty willing to help move through war to peace. All of the good days as a leader had prepared me for the bad times. The way that I handled issues when they were small was indicative of how I would handle the war and the support I would receive. A good leader understands that she cannot do it all, so she surrounds herself with a team of people who can be reliable and effective. Surviving a war is not about who has more might, but who has the fortitude to last. One person cannot last alone, but a group with a common mission and strong leadership can endure.

So . . . the process moved forward. We were a little bruised as a division, but our department emerged stronger. Not because we had more space, but because we had forged a bond of support that we did not allow anyone to damage. We were never more focused on our goals and supporting each other than we were at that time. It marked the beginning of a new period of cohesiveness. As never before, we were one unit, all different people but the same. And at the end of the day, we were an incredible team. Because we moved forward in peace, everyone has moved forward. The only way to survive a war is to move through and never let it get in the way of future success.

# Values and Purpose at the Core

Anita Wells, PhD

Purpose and meaning are essential to success and to making a difference in the lives of others. My parents and grandparents taught me this, and the relevance of that credo to leadership becomes clearer to me with each challenge and opportunity I encounter. My father and mother stressed that my siblings and I should strive to leave the world, in some measure, better than we found it; doing so is nearly impossible without purpose. My family used the language of values and demonstrated that identifying the beliefs and establishing the practices that form the foundation of who I am as a person, how I treat others, and the decisions I make would provide a compass for me during times of change and controversy. Core values open the door to purpose and meaning and purpose undergirds goals. My family's legacy of service resonates in Barsh and Cranston's (2011c) statement that:

> Goals that transcend the self—goals that serve other people, a cause or a community—have the greatest impact on your sense of fulfillment. At the same time, to be meaningful, goals must be highly personal: They must inpire you to take on greater challenges and growth.

Among my core values are fairness and respect, compassion and loyalty, integrity and humility. Each of these is important to how I understand the world.

I am the middle child of three and grew up in a household

with two parents whose love for each other was evident, even in the midst of tension. I loved my older brother and younger sister then as now, and would, with genuine conviction, speak up for and defend them if they seemed to be unfairly chastised or punished; this willingness to speak my mind sometimes landed me in trouble, yet, my behavior remained consistent. As a child, I was a talker, an explainer. Though my desire to understand others and be understood was often trying to my mother, she always knew where I stood and knew that I would honor my word; this engendered trust between us.

Unkindness toward or exclusion of others was always intolerable to me; I noticed when people were on the margins and reached out. My parents and my Quaker education emphasized that "there is that of God in everyone" which, in part, meant that status and position make no one of us better than another and that I should always treat others as I would want to be treated.

As I continue to develop in leadership, I reflect periodically on the concept of lifelong learning emphasized by Schein (2010) and the notion that each of us has the capacity to be a life-long learner. Schein's emphasis is especially relevant for faculty and leaders in academic environments in which we spend a great deal of time teaching and training others. I took advantage of an opportunity to study leadership through a postgraduate academic leadership certificate program with other women of color working at historically black colleges and universities. Through the program I increased my network of supportive collaborative professional women of color, increased my *carpe diem* capacity, became more fully aware of my professional value, and began to claim my worth. I encourage women of color, especially, to seek developmental and collaborative experiences with like peers

---

and to have mentors and a sponsor. There is no doubt that frank feedback, encouragement, and knowledge from those more experienced than I am has been and continues to be invaluable.

I learned that the model of leadership geared toward the betterment of society with which I grew up both at home and in school has a name and that it is, appropriately, termed servant leadership (Greenleaf, 2010). I learned that the top-down model of leadership, motivated by task accomplishment, which persists as the most common form of leadership and which was promoted and rewarded in many of my post-secondary educational and work environments is termed *transactional leadership*. Throughout my academic and professional careers I have found myself influenced greatly by this model while still drawn to and operating with the values associated with the servant leadership model. Bass and Riggio (2010) noted that the transformational model, which continues to gain prominence and which emphasizes empowering others and two-way communication, can be difficult for individuals and organizations to adopt. I am drawn to the model's motivation to empower others and am also cognizant that even when operating within a transformational model the ability and willingness to make a unilateral decision may be required.

I highly value relationships and the benefits of genuine mutual respect, of closeness with others, and of the opportunity to care for other people. Relationships are at the heart of many of my values and have a tremendous impact on my work and personal life and how I structure my priorities. This relational approach continues to inform my leadership development. Eagly and Carli (2007) described differences between democratic/participative and autocratic/directive leadership styles and indicate that research shows that women tend to be more democratic/ participative than men.

In my early twenties, after I completed college, I found myself caring for my paternal grandmother who was quite ill. During this time, I learned that I could be decisive in high-stakes situations, that I could exercise respectful authority in relationship with others (the bank, the pharmacy, nurses' aides, the health insurance company) and "get the job done." During this time, I also worked for a large corporation. The company downsized during my tenure and I witnessed the pain of misplaced loyalty and the shifting landscape of employment as some people, after 20 years of service, were let go, in some instances with no notice. This experience led me to ask myself, were I in charge of an organization that was in financial difficulty and/or acquiring another organization, how would I go about making decisions that affect the lives of others? How could I exercise fairness and respect, demonstrate compassion and humility? I didn't have ready answers, but I began then to think about what it means to be in positions of power and authority and be responsible for others.

Positions I have held and the work I have done—from directing outreach for a nonprofit organization to project management on various research endeavors to management of a graduate program—have strengthened my belief in the importance of integrity. I have grown more comfortable with being the lone voice when I am grounded in the integrity of the stance I am taking. My experiences in supervising a staff of 15 employees, leading teams of colleagues, and coordinating groups of students, have reinforced the importance of communicating and taking into account what is communicated to me. I believe that, in order to lead, one has to understand how to be an effective follower, how to listen and take direction humbly from others who are in the best position to give it. I have learned that it is vital to acknowledge the contributions of others, publicly when appropriate, to apologize when I have wronged someone or misunderstood a situation and acted on that misunderstanding, and to show appreciation; doing so takes nothing from you and often increases morale and productivity. Learning from experience is not always easy; recognition of "when new behaviors, skills or attitudes are called for which involves being able to see when current approaches are not working" (Val Velsor & Guthrie, 1998, p. 243) is key.

Gender, race and culture are important variables in how a woman is perceived in all settings, including professional work environments. What Davis and Maldonado (2015) discussed as the intersection of race and gender has without doubt had an influence on my leadership development. As a black woman I am keenly aware of both my race and my gender in situations in which my role is to follow and in those in which it is to lead. I have experienced discrimination at the behest of both men and women. Across my education and professional work life I have experienced being underestimated due to my race and being underpaid due to my gender as well as been the recipient of racist and sexist commentary, part of the double jeopardy of race and gender (Davis & Maldonado, 2015). For example, I was a strong student in high school and civically engaged in activities I enjoyed. When I was admitted to several top colleges I was told by white male peers that I had taken their spots. Also, I was once asked to make a case for why I should be chosen for a job over a white female counterpart who was less qualified than I both in education and experience; when I received the promotion a memo was sent out without consultation and with my full résumé attached as if to explain my selection. Similarly, I was told by a female supervisor that I was not director material, though I was simultaneously relied upon to direct myself in the management of an entity for which I developed policies and procedures, strategized for continued growth, and formed relationships with other units, all of which enabled the entity's success and continuation. Unfortunately, none of these experiences are unique and some are quite familiar to many women of color. These types of experiences as well as the regular microaggressions discussed by Holder, Jackson, and Ponterotto (2015) can have a cumulative detrimental effect over time on self-efficacy and esteem. On the heels of some of these experiences, I struggled at times with feeling unsure of myself and my ability. Though undeniably painful, through these experiences I learned about myself, about adaptive methods of coping with adversity and confronting conflict, and about how I would not want to treat others.

In their research examining the coping mechanisms of black women who are leaders in corporate settings and dealing with microaggressions, Holder, Jackson, and Ponterotto (2015) found, among other things, that black women utilized things such as support networks of like peers, religion and spirituality, and armoring. Similarly, I have learned the wisdom of not adopting others' attitudes toward and opinions of me whether positive or negative; to do so is to position your house on shifting sand. Additionally, as a clinician, I am reminded that negativity and unconstructive criticism from others is sometimes borne of insecurity, a basic lack of self-satisfaction or unattended pain, none of which ought to be employed (consciously or unconsciously) to undermine another. Through listening and observing others whose leadership I admire I continue to hone my own style and practice.

My training in research, the science of psychology, and clinical psychology each emphasized in different ways the tenets of emotional intelligence including self-awareness, empathy, self-regulation, and motivation (Goleman, 1998). Self-awareness and empathy can aid a strong leader in developing an appropriate humility, by increasing her capacity to better understand others and learn from her mistakes. Failure is valuable; I often learn as much if not more from my failures as from my successes. Dyer, Gregersen, and Christensen (2009) talk about this phenomenon in their discussion of the usefulness of failure in inspiring innovation in an organization or society. I have found that when I acknowledge my failures and assess what and where I went wrong, I see ideas and alternatives I did not before and am further encouraged in compassion for others. The ability to care for another human being and their concerns as if they were your own can enable a leader to increase her knowledge of others, anticipate problems, and engender trust in those she is leading. Similarly, self-regulation, which enables one to have a reasonable and considered response to others (Goleman, 1998) is key to building trust and loyalty and, when coupled with self-awareness, can lead to empowering others. As a leader I hope always to contribute to the strengthening of environments in which honesty and integrity are practiced and valued, and in which asking questions and debating issues is not only encouraged and without repercussion but is used to move an institution forward.

The deeper meaning of leadership for me is living a life that demonstrates my belief in God through the integrity I evidence, the compassion and fairness I demonstrate, the encouragement I offer others and myself, and the humility I experience and embody. Authentic leadership to me means honesty, leading for purpose, and cultivating processes and individuals that are skilled and confident such that, were I to leave today, the entity I led will thrive tomorrow. Liang (2010) conducted interviews with five of the top emerging leaders. One of her questions was: What is the single most important piece of advice you would give to emerging leaders? My answer to that question today is: Identify and hold fast to your core values. They will guide and ground you in the midst of challenge and triumph, will remind you of your worth and gifts when you and others doubt, and will enable you to best serve and inspire others from a position of strength.

# References

Barsh, J., & Cranston, S. (2011). *How remarkable women lead: The breakthrough model for work and life.* Crown Business: New York,.

Bass, B. M., & Riggio, R. E. (2010). The transformational model of leadership. In G. R. Hickman (Ed.), *Leading organizations: Perspectives for a new era* (2nd ed.), pp. 87-95. Thousand Oaks, CA: Sage Publications, Inc.

Davis, D. R., & Maldonado, C. (2015). Shattering the glass ceiling: The leadership development of African American women in higher education. *Advancing Women in Leadership* (35), 48-64.

Dyer, J. H., Gregersen, H. B., & Christensen, C.M. (2009). The innovator's DNA: Five "discovery skills" separate true innovators from the rest of us. *Harvard Business Review*, December, 61-67.

Eagly, A. H., & Carli, L. L. (2007). *Through the labyrinth: The truth about how women become leaders.* Boston, MA: Harvard Business School Press._

Goleman, D. (1998). What makes a leader? *Harvard Business Review*. Republished January 2004 in Best of Harvard Business Review, 82-91.

Greenleaf, R. K. (2010). Servant leadership. In G. R. Hickman (Ed.), *Leading organizations: Perspectives for a new era* (2nd ed.), pp. 87-95. Thousand Oaks, CA: Sage Publications, Inc.

Holder, A.M.B., Jackson, M. A., & Ponterotto, J. G. (2015). Racial microaggression experiences and coping strategies of black women in corporate leadership. *Qualitative Psychology* (2), 160-180.

Liang, L. (2010). Leading through the fog: Leadership secrets from five top emerging leaders. *Diversity MBA Magazine*. Retrieved 9/20/2013 from http://diversitymbamagazine.com/leading-through-the-fog-leadership-secrets-from-five-top-emerging-leaders.

Schein, E. H. (2010). The learning culture and the learning leader. In G. R. Hickman (Ed.), *Leading organizations: Perspectives for a new era* (2nd ed.), pp. 331-344. Thousand Oaks, CA: Sage Publications, Inc.

Van Velsor, E., & Guthrie, V. A. (1998). Enhancing the ability to learn from experience. In C.D. McCauley, R. S. Moxley, & E. Van Velsor (Eds.), *The Center for Creative Leadership handbook of leadership development* (1st ed.), pp.

242-261. San Francisco, CA: Jossey-Bass.

# About the Authors

**Dr. Olga Bolden-Tiller** is an Associate Professor of Animal Science and Head of the Department of Agricultural and Environmental Sciences at Tuskegee University. She holds a BS degree in Agricultural Sciences (Animal Sciences) from Fort Valley State University (1997) and a PhD degree in Animal Sciences (Reproductive Biology) from the University of Missouri-Columbia, where she matriculated as a USDA-National Needs Fellow. Following her graduate work, Dr. Bolden-Tiller continued her training at the University of Texas-MD Anderson Cancer Center as an NIH Fellow in Reproductive Biology (2002-2005). Her research interests include elucidating the molecular mechanisms of ovarian and testicular function, as well as specifically mechanisms that regulate spermatogenesis and the effect of various factors, including nutrition and synthetic microbial peptides, on ovarian and testicular function in rodents and ruminants. Her research and training programs are funded by the United States Department of Agriculture, the National Science Foundation, and the State of Alabama (Alabama Agricultural Land Grant Alliance). She is the author/co-author of numerous refereed journal articles and conference proceedings and is an active member of numerous professional societies, serving in leadership roles in many, including the American Society of Animal Sciences and the Society for the Study of Reproduction, as well as Minorities in Agriculture, Natural Resources and Related Sciences. Dr. Bolden-Tiller has received several awards, including the TU College of Agriculture, Environmental and Natural Sciences' Faculty Performance Award for Service (2008) and Teaching (2010) as well as the Russell Brown Distinguished Scientist Award (2013).

**Dr. Kimarie Engerman** received her PhD in Educational Psychology from Howard University. She completed a postdoc in Engineering Education at the Center for the Advancement of Engineering Education. Dr. Engerman also participated in the Quality Education for Minorities, Leadership Development Institute. She has served as principal investigator and co-principal investigator on various grants. While participating in the OURS Program, Dr. Engerman was promoted to Associate Professor of Psychology at the University of the Virgin Islands. Additionally, she became a provost fellow and held the following leadership positions: Interim Dean for the College of Liberal Arts and Social Sciences; Chair, Academic Advising Committee; Chair, Dual Credit Committee; Chair, Institutional Review Board; Developer and Coordinator, Junior Faculty Mentoring Program; and Coordinator, Faculty Development Writing Group. Dr. Engerman's Action Learning Project (ALP) on academic advising, completed as part of the requirement for the OURS Program, was the focus of the 2014 university-wide Faculty Institute. As a result of her ALP, the academic advising culture has changed at the University of the Virgin Islands.

**Bianca L. Garner, PhD** is a Professor of Biology at Tougaloo College. She received a BS in chemistry from Xavier University of Louisiana, a MS in microbiology from the University of South Florida and a PhD from the University of Mississippi Medical Center. She has been the recipient of more than $1 million in extramural funding for undergraduate support, serving as the co-PI of the National Science Foundation's (NSF) HBCU-UP and S-STEM. She has received several research grants, including a NSF Molecular and Cellular Biology Investigator Initiated Award and the Mississippi National Institutes of Health (NIH) INBRE. Dr. Garner has served as a grant reviewer for NSF and the American Colleges and University's Project Kaleidoscope. She is also a journal reviewer for MDPI Pathogens and Toxins. She is currently a fellow of the NIH Programs to Increase Diversity Among Individuals Engaged in Health-Related Research Functional and Translational Genomics of Blood Disorders. Dr. Garner's administrative positions include Assistant Dean and Chair of the Biology Department.

**Amber B. Hodges, PhD** is an Associate Professor in the Department of Psychology at Morgan State University. Her current research examines factors and barriers impacting STEM efficacy and persistence in minority students. Dr. Hodges was a fellow in the Leadership Development Institute supported by the Quality Education for Minority Network and the National Science Foundation. Additionally, she earned a Post-Graduate Certificate in Academic Leadership from the Chicago School of Professional Psychology through the Opportunities for Underrepresented Scholars program funded by the National Science Foundation. Dr. Hodges earned her PhD in Psychology from the Graduate School and University Center, the City University of New York (CUNY). She holds an M.Phil in Psychology from the Graduate School and University Center, CUNY, and a B.S. in Psychology from Bennett College. She recently coauthored a chapter describing successful mentoring models undergirded by psychology theories.

**Linda Johnson, PhD** is Associate Professor of Biology in the Department of Natural Sciences at the University of Maryland Eastern Shore (UMES). Dr. Johnson received a B.A. in Chemistry at Lincoln University, Pennsylvania in 1985. She completed her graduate studies at Temple University School of Medicine in Philadelphia, where she first obtained a M.S. in Biochemistry in 1989 and then a PhD in Anatomy and Cell Biology in 1995. She continued her research in molecular reproductive biology as a postdoctoral fellow and later as a research associate at the University of Pennsylvania School of Medicine. In 1999, she joined UMES as an Assistant Professor of Biology, where she was promoted and granted tenure in 2005. While broadening her research efforts, Dr. Johnson also expanded her interests to student and faculty development. Through the many roles Dr. Johnson played at her institution including instructor, mentor, advisor, chair, director, PI, and committee member, she has had significant successes in increasing the number of underrepresented students who matriculated into medical and doctoral degree programs. In addition, through many of those same roles, Dr. Johnson has played a significant role in the development and advancement of many UMES faculty members, particularly women of color.

**Dr. Jumoke Oluwakemi Ladeji-Osias** is Associate Professor in the Department of Electrical and Computer Engineering at Morgan State University in Baltimore, where she teaches undergraduate and graduate courses in computer engineering. Dr. Ladeji-Osias earned a B.S. in electrical engineering from the University of Maryland, College Park, a PhD in biomedical engineering from Rutgers, the State University of New Jersey, and a Post-Graduate Certificate in Academic Leadership from the Chicago School of Professional Psychology (Cohort I). Since completion of the OURS program, she has focused on multi-institution research collaborations and co-organized a national workshop on credentialing design competencies in engineering in April, 2016. Dr. Ladeji-Osias conducts research in embedded security for the Internet of Things, broadening participation of underrepresented minorities in engineering and K-12 STEM education. Her work is primarily funded by the National Science Foundation and the Verizon Foundation. She serves on the Advisory Committee for the Middle Atlantic Section of the American Society for Engineering Education and as an ABET Program Evaluator for the Engineering Accreditation Commission (EAC) representing IEEE. She enjoys observing the intellectual and professional growth in students as they prepare for engineering careers.

**Dr. Stephanie Luster-Teasley** is an associate professor with a joint appointment in the Department of Civil, Architectural and Environmental Engineering and the Department of Chemical, Biological and Bioengineering at North Carolina A&T State University. Her research specializations include environmental remediation, water sustainability, and engineering education. She is currently the Director for the North Carolina A&T Engage2BE Engineers strengths-based mentoring and scholarship program. Funded by the Department of Education, this program is specifically designed to provide support for under-represented, low-income students with children and students with disabilities interested in pursuing engineering careers and graduate school. Additionally, Dr. Luster-Teasley serves as a co-PI for the NCA&T ADVANCE grant, has received funding from the National Science Foundation to develop and implement case studies modules to improve critical thinking in laboratory instruction, and funding from private foundations to implement science programs for K-12 minority students. Overall, her disciplinary, science education research, and professional development grants have yielded over $6,500,000 in funding.

**Dr. Michel A. Reece** is currently an associate professor and research director of the Center of Microwave, Satellite, and RF Engineering (COM-SARE) in the Department of Electrical and Computer Engineering at Morgan State University. In this center, she pursues research in the areas of high-frequency device characterization and modeling, RF/ MMIC circuit design, highly efficient solid-state power amplifier networks, and adaptable electronic components for software-defined radio applications. She became the first female recipient at Morgan State to obtain her doctorate degree in Engineering in 2003. She received her B.S. from Morgan State in 1995 and her M.S.E.E. from Penn State in 1997, both in Electrical Engineering. Previously, she served as a postdoctoral researcher in the Microwave Systems Section of the RF Engineering Group at Johns Hopkins University's Applied Physics Laboratory Space Department. She has a passion for education, where she has developed curriculum for the RF Microwave Engineering concentration offered at MSU, the only HBCU to have a dedicated program in this area. She has also taught as an adjunct faculty member at Johns Hopkins University's Engineering Professionals Program.

**Dr. Tamara Rogers** received her PhD in Electrical Engineering from Vanderbilt University. Her dissertation was entitled "The Human Agent: A model for human-robot interaction" and investigated features of social interaction for a humanoid robot and task performance. She is currently an Associate Professor in the Department of Computer Science at Tennessee State University in Nashville, Tennessee. Dr. Rogers has a passion for teaching and engaging students for learning. Eager to be effective in these pursuits, her participation in projects such as the NSF Opportunities for UnderRepresented Scholars (OURS) program and Preparing Critical Faculty for the Future (PCFF) have helped her to develop skills and encourage others as well. She is currently serving as the Graduate Program Coordinator for the Master of Science in Computer Science program at TSU. In addition, she advises undergraduate students in academics, student projects, and the TSU student ACM chapter. She is currently working in the research areas of cyber security and networking, including coaching the Cyber Challenge team.

**Dr. Suzanne Seleem**, **PhD** is a Chair and Associate Professor at Central State University. She received her BSc in Chemistry at American University, her MSc in Materials Engineering at American University, and her PhD in Chemistry at the University of W. London. She has been chair of the Natural Sciences Department since 2009. She has chaired the CSU IRB committee, as well as several committees for the Rotary International Organization. Her research is currently concentrated on heavy metal analysis in hair products as well as inhibition reactions and polymer formations. She is CSU PI on an ADVANCE grant funded by the NSF and has participated in many grants funded by the NIH, DOD, and DOE. She would like to lead an institutional effort in faculty development as VP of academic development.

**Dr. Gloria Thomas** serves as Executive Director of Research, Education and Mentoring Programs in the Office of Strategic Initiatives at Louisiana State University (LSU), with oversight of education, mentoring, and diversity programs in science, technology, engineering, and mathematics (STEM) across the K-12 to graduate student levels. She received a bachelor's degree in chemistry from Southern University and A&M College, where she held scholarships from the Timbuktu Academy, the Honors College, and the Packard Foundation. Thomas was a National Research Council Postdoctoral Fellow at the National Institute of Standards and Technology and an Assistant Professor at Mississippi State University and Xavier University of Louisiana. Dr. Thomas is passionate about STEM education and broadening the participation of underrepresented groups. She received the 2014 Excellence in Mentoring Award, the 2010 Henry McBay Award for Excellence in Teaching, and the 2008 Outstanding Service Award, all from the National Organization of Black Chemists and Chemical Engineers. She also earned the 2007 Stanley C. Israel Award for Advancing Diversity in the Chemical Sciences from the American Chemical Society.

**Dr. C. Ellen Washington** holds a PhD in Industrial Organizational Psychology. She is the Assistant Director of Leadership Development and Scholar-in-Residence at North Carolina State University in Raleigh, North Carolina. She also serves as Adjunct Faculty for the Shelton Leadership Institute at NC State. Previously she served seven years as Chair of the Department of Psychology and Chair of the IRB Committee at Saint Augustine's University in Raleigh. Dr. Washington completed the OURS Fellowship at the Chicago School of Professional Psychology, where she earned a postdoc certificate in Academic Leadership. Dr. Washington offers significant experience in academic leadership, women in leadership, higher educational learning models, strategic planning, change management, and organizational development.

**Dr. Clytrice Watson** is a Professor of Biology and the Interim Dean for the College of Mathematics, Natural Sciences and Technology at Delaware State University. Dr. Watson received her bachelor's degree in Biology from Norfolk State University, her master's degree from Delaware State University, and her PhD from the University of Maryland Eastern Shore. She also completed a certificate of Academic Leadership via the OURS (Opportunities for UnderRepresented Scholars) graduate certificate program at the Chicago School of Professional Psychology. She is committed to serving her community, as she currently serves on the Delaware Commission for Forensic Science and the board of Directors of Delaware-Bio, and participates in educational outreach programs across and outside the state. Her personal commitment to student mentoring and academic success stems from her personal experiences of having excellent mentors throughout her academic and professional career.

 **Dr. Anita Wells** is an assistant professor in the Department of Psychology at Morgan State University, where she serves as the Graduate Program Coordinator for the master's and PhD programs in Psychometrics and a voting member of the Graduate Council of the University. She was selected in 2013 to be a fellow in the inaugural cohort of the National Science Foundation Opportunities for Underrepresented Scholars (NSF/OURS) Academic Leadership Certificate Program at the Chicago School of Professional Psychology, Washington, DC. Dr. Wells earned her PhD in Clinical Psychology at Northwestern University's Feinberg School of Medicine. She completed the majority of her clinical training with the Department of Veterans Affairs, including an internship at Hines VA Hospital in Illinois. She completed postdoctoral training with the Kellogg Health Scholars Program Postdoctoral Fellowship in Health Disparities at Morgan State University and Johns Hopkins University. Dr. Wells also holds a master's in psychology from Wesleyan University and a bachelor's degree in African American studies from Yale University.

**Dr. Leyte Winfield** is a teacher, mentor, and scholar dedicated to nurturing potential and empowering agency in women of African descent pursuing careers in STEM. She has been on faculty at Spelman College since 2003. During this time, she has established a research program that investigates the relationship between the structure of a molecule, particularly benzimidazoles, and its utility as a therapeutic agent against breast, ovarian, and prostate cancers. Her research has been recognized by the American Association of Cancer Research and the Council for Undergraduate Research and has been funded in part by the National Institutes of Health (NIH) and the National Science Foundation (NSF). As Chair of the Department of Chemistry & Biochemistry at Spelman College, she has built upon the strength of the department's past success to establish new strategies for structured curricular reform. She is currently leading the department's efforts to broaden the curriculum to meet the ideals of a liberal arts education while simultaneously providing students with resources that promote improved engagement and performance in their majors. Dr.Winfield's record of leadership has included service as Interim Associate Provost of Research as well as directorships of the NSF-funded HBCU-UP ASPIRE, the ExxonMobil WISE Scholars, the NIH-funded Women of Color Legacy (WCL), and the endowed Department of Chemistry & Biochemistry Scholars programs. These activities reflect programmatic efforts geared towards improving diversity in STEM.

**Dr. Yolander R. Youngblood** is currently an Assistant Professor of Biology and Co-ordinator of the Biology Research Symposium at Prairie View A and M University in Prairie View, Texas. She received her PhD in Botany from the University of Florida. Since 2014, Dr. Youngblood has used her National Science Foundation – Opportunities for Underrepresented Scholars (NSF-OURS) leadership training to increase the number of undergraduates in her laboratory, completed two additional science publications, applied for additional grants, and successfully expanded and broadened the participation of students and faculty in the Biology Research Symposium (to be held each Fall semester). In Spring 2016, she was inducted as a member of Sigma Xi, the Scientific Research Society. Membership is by invitation only.

# About Fielding Graduate University

Fielding Graduate University, headquartered in Santa Barbara, CA, was founded in 1974, and celebrated its 40th anniversary in 2014. Fielding is an accredited, nonprofit leader in blended graduate education, combining face-to-face and online learning. Its curriculum offers quality master's and doctoral degrees for professionals and academics around the world. Fielding's faculty members represent a wide spectrum of scholarship and practice in the fields of educational leadership, human and organizational development, and clinical and media psychology. Fielding's faculty serves as mentors and guides to self-directed students who use their skills and professional experience to become powerful, socially responsible leaders in their communities, workplaces, and society. For more information, please visit Fielding online at www.fielding.edu.

Made in United States
North Haven, CT
21 May 2022

19384829R00107